The Horses We Love, The Lessons We Learn

Tena Bastian

BICENTENNIAL
1807
WILEY
2007
BICENTENNIAL

Wiley Publishing, Inc.

Howell Book House
Published by Wiley Publishing, Inc., Hoboken, New Jersey

No part of this publication may be reproduced, stored in a retrieval system or transmitted in any form or by any means, electronic, mechanical, photocopying, recording, scanning or otherwise, except as permitted under Sections 107 or 108 of the 1976 United States Copyright Act, without either the prior written permission of the Publisher, or authorization through payment of the appropriate per-copy fee to the Copyright Clearance Center, 222 Rosewood Drive, Danvers, MA 01923, (978) 750-8400, fax (978) 646-8600, or on the web at www.copyright.com. Requests to the Publisher for permission should be addressed to the Legal Department, Wiley Publishing, Inc., 10475 Crosspoint Blvd., Indianapolis, IN 46256, (317) 572-3447, fax (317) 572-4355, or online at http://www.wiley.com/go/permissions.

Wiley, the Wiley Publishing logo, Howell Book House, and related trademarks are trademarks or registered trademarks of John Wiley & Sons, Inc. and/or its affiliates. All other trademarks are the property of their respective owners. Wiley Publishing, Inc. is not associated with any product or vendor mentioned in this book.

The publisher and the author make no representations or warranties with respect to the accuracy or completeness of the contents of this work and specifically disclaim all warranties, including without limitation warranties of fitness for a particular purpose. No warranty may be created or extended by sales or promotional materials. The advice and strategies contained herein may not be suitable for every situation. This work is sold with the understanding that the publisher is not engaged in rendering legal, accounting, or other professional services. If professional assistance is required, the services of a competent professional person should be sought. Neither the publisher nor the author shall be liable for damages arising here from. The fact that an organization or Website is referred to in this work as a citation and/or a potential source of further information does not mean that the author or the publisher endorses the information the organization or Website may provide or recommendations it may make. Further, readers should be aware that Internet Websites listed in this work may have changed or disappeared between when this work was written and when it is read.

Although these stories are true, some names have been changed for privacy purposes. Any other similarities to any person either alive or deceased are purely coincidental.

For general information on our other products and services or to obtain technical support please contact our Customer Care Department within the U.S. at (800) 762-2974, outside the U.S. at (317) 572-3993 or fax (317) 572-4002.

Wiley also publishes its books in a variety of electronic formats. Some content that appears in print may not be available in electronic books. For more information about Wiley products, please visit our web site at www.wiley.com.

Library of Congress Cataloging-in-Publication Data
Bastian, Tena.
  The horses we love, the lessons we learn / Tena Bastian.
    p. cm.
  ISBN-13: 978-0-470-11425-4 (pbk. : alk. paper)
  ISBN-10: 0-470-11425-8
  1. Horses—Anecdotes. 2. Horsemen and horsewomen—Anecdotes. 3. Horsemanship—Anecdotes. 4. Human-animal relationships—Anecdotes. I. Title.
  SF301.B37 2007
  636.1—dc22
                          2006036943

Printed in the United States of America

10 9 8 7 6 5 4 3 2

Book design by LeAndra Hosier
Book production by Wiley Publishing, Inc. Composition Services

Tell me a story, Daddy
About when you were young
Sing to me a song
That your Mama might have sung
When she rocked you in your cradle
Did she sing you lullabies
Before the bough breaks, Daddy
I need to see you through her eyes

Describe to me a million stars
On a long hot summer night
Hold me like you used to
And make everything all right
Tell me about the porch swing
Your old dog, the people you would meet
Tell me again how you would walk to school
With no shoes upon your feet

Did you go to church on Sunday
Did you sit in the very first pew
Please, tell me a story, Daddy
About the horses that you knew
When you bowed your head and prayed to God
Did he hear your prayers somehow
Tell me the words that you used to say
Because I need to repeat them now

Just tell me one more story
Before you close your eyes
And I will hold you in my heart forever
No tears, no sad goodbyes
Every story you leave behind
Through every memory
I will come to know just who I am
By the boy you used to be

I will share every story
From the first word to the last
I will find my faith through your belief
My future through your past
And when your life is over
It will be your legacy
Tell me a story, Daddy
And you will live on through me.

In Loving Memory of my father, Ellis Ward Coker "Pawdaddy"

Table of Contents

Acknowledgments

To my husband, Bear, for all the years that he has loved me beyond my greatest expectation.

To Dusty, Jennifer, and Garrett, for filling my life with laughter, love, and hope for the future.

To Lynn Northrup, for her editing expertise. To Courtney Doss at Wrangler Corporation, who dresses me in style even when I am quite content in my pajama pants and old hoodies. To Kate Epstein, my agent, for always understanding my creative process of thinking.

To the entire horse industry for supporting us through the most difficult time in our lives.

To Jacci Moss, Dr. Cindy Thurston, and all the volunteers at Friends of Felines and Earth Angels in Defiance, Ohio.

In loving memory of Rex Wiley, Jack Osgerby, Mr. Metcalf, and Patience Prebeg Haas.

To my mom, dad, and brothers and sisters for giving me roots; and to God for giving me wings and faith enough to believe that all things are possible.

Pawdaddy—boxes of photos, endless stories, morning talks, and a father who loved me. My life is perfect and I will miss you.

About the Author

Known to many for her work as a Western poet, Tena Bastian is a previously published author and clinician. She has presented seminars at Equine Affaire in Ohio, Kentucky, and California; as well as at the Western States Horse Expo, the North American Horse Spectacular, and the South Dakota Horse Fair, to name a few.

Tena has been involved with horses for most of her life. She and her husband own a small ranch in Ohio, where they raise, train, and breed horses, including three-time world-qualifying Palomino stallion, This Beau's Eligible. Tena's previous book, *The Foal is the Goal: Managing Your Mare and Handling a Stallion,* was published by Trafalgar Square Publishing. Her poem, "Iron Horse," was released on a limited-edition print and was featured in several major equine magazines. The original was auctioned at the All American Quarter Horse Congress to raise money for the North American Riding for the Handicapped Association (NARHA). You can contact Tena at www.tenabastian.com.

Introduction

Every morning, when I walk out to my barn, I am given a gift. Whether it is the soft, familiar nicker of an old friend or the excitement of meeting the newest resident, it is a precious gift that I know I will treasure for the rest of my life. It doesn't make any difference how bad my day is going, the next morning when it is quiet and I begin a new day, I go out to my barn, and all is right with the world. Likewise, every person that we meet in our lives is a gift.

Each of us has the ability to change a life every, single day. We have the power to make someone smile just by how we greet that person. I believe in a universal subconscious, and I believe that each of us contributes to it in a way that can change the energy of the entire world. If we greet all the people we meet with a smile and a kind word, it sets off a spark in them that they pass along to others. The recent events in the world have created such a negativity within the universal subconscious that it makes it extremely difficult to face the challenges in our lives. I have learned through experience that horses can teach us so much about ourselves and how we view the world around us. It is in that perception that we can strive to make our lives, and the lives that we touch, more fulfilling.

Horses are incredibly perceptive, and this is their first similarity to human beings. They have taught me that if I enter that barn with a negative attitude, I am going to get negativity back, and I am going to be responsible for setting the mood for my entire day. So every morning when I enter my barn, I do so with the same excitement that should be applied to the beginning of everyone's day. These creatures of God give me the gift of understanding human nature through the study of animal behavior. This is an important lesson that I learned very early on and over the years, it has developed into something so much more than I ever imagined. It has gotten me through the most difficult times in my life. Begin every day of your life with excitement and anticipation of all that is possible and all that is yours to enjoy, and this positive approach will come back to you tenfold.

This is the first of many gifts that I will share with you throughout this book. I will introduce you to horses that have taught me so many lessons that make life a little easier; simple things such as this that will change your life and teach you how to deal with the challenges that you face. I always try to appreciate this gift. My family and I are privileged to have learned so much from the horses and the horse people that we have known and loved.

It is said that experience is the best teacher, and I believe this to be true. I also believe that learning from others' experiences is just as important. I want to share with you some of the knowledge I have gained from my experiences in a way that will be entertaining. I will tell you stories of some incredibly amazing horses that I have had the privilege of knowing and loving, and tell you how each of them has taught me about the important issues in my life. The basic principles that I have learned from these horses may give you a better insight into understanding the people that you meet. It is my hope that, because of these stories, you will see your life in an entirely different light. It begins today with a simple act of kindness. Greet all people that you meet, regardless of how difficult they may seem, with a positive attitude. Say hello, make eye contact, smile and when they ask you how you are, tell them that today is the best day of your life. Even if it isn't a particularly great day, if you feed the universal subconscious with positive thought, it will be.

Finding Joy

People love horses, and I have come to understand why. They have the purest of souls, and their forgiveness of our mistakes is never-ending. At times, I almost believe that they understand life better than I ever have. They see the world in an entirely fresh perspective, with a childlike view that we have managed to lose over the years. I can still remember waking up on a summer morning genuinely excited about going outside to play. At some point in my life, with the pressures of being an adult and the worries of trying to keep up in a fast-paced world, I lost the ability to enjoy the simple pleasure of going outside to play. Horses never lose that excitement. I can walk even the oldest of horses out to a nice, green pasture on a warm summer morning, and the moment I release them, they run and kick up their heels and roll in the wet grass and play tag along the fence line. They remind you of the importance of enjoying things such as a warm summer morning, and they remind you to play. You have to find that child inside of you and remember how to play once in a while. You have to be a horse and run and kick up your heels. You have to put all of your troubles aside and just have fun. Schedule time for yourself and do something so utterly silly that you laugh out loud and do it just for the sake of exercising your inner child.

When horses work, most of them find joy in their work, which is something we tend to lose because we work in a world that is so incredibly competitive. They find ways to keep it fresh and enjoyable. The secret that horses have taught me about enjoying work is to find a new approach and change my schedule now and then to avoid getting in a rut. Don't judge your performance by the standards of others but rather by your own personal goals. If you did a task better than you did it the last time, you are making progress. Horses do not schedule competitive events; people do. We schedule horse shows where we compete against each other—honestly, our horses could care less how the other horses are doing, they simply try in an effort to please us. They would be just as content going on a trail ride in the park. Of course, there are exceptions, just as there are with people. Some horses have a natural competitive nature and insist on being the fastest or the strongest. They enjoy pushing themselves beyond normal limits and succeeding at whatever they do. What these horses teach us is that when we push ourselves too hard, we usually burn out quickly. Work hard but enjoy your work and pace yourself, and you will be happier as a result. Above all else, don't forget to find the balance between work and play.

A horse's curiosity never ceases to amaze me. A horse can find joy in the simplest of things that we have come to ignore. I have laid in a hammock out in a pasture full of horses and watched one of them follow a bird that walked through the green grass for several feet before the bird took wing and flew away. I have ridden my horse through a state park and have humored him in his curiosity to pursue a deer.

Be curious about the simple things. Learn for the pure sake of learning and always seek to expand on what you know. Revisit the simple things that you have come to ignore and appreciate them again.

Genetics and Environment

From the time a horse is born, every action or reaction to which he is exposed affects that horse in some way. I believe that the two main factors that govern a horse's overall personality are his genetic makeup and his environment. By genetics, I not only mean the breed of any given horse but also the tendencies within each breed.

Just as the color or height or any other physical trait is decided by the genetic makeup of each horse, personality traits are linked to genetics as well. For instance, the disposition of a foal born to a sire and a dam that are relatively easygoing will most likely be easygoing. A foal born to high-spirited parents is likely to take on that same disposition. There are certainly exceptions to this rule, but genetics play a large part in each horse's personality and disposition. Genetically speaking, it isn't that different with people.

From the day a horse is born, the environment in which it is raised will have a distinct impact on the horse's overall personality. The same holds true for people. Every action that a parent takes with a child, and every reaction that a parent displays in any given situation, is going to affect that child. Likewise, every action that a handler takes with her horse, and every reaction that the handler displays to any given situation, is going to affect that horse. Everything horses experience in their surroundings will make a difference as well; this is why it is so important to create an environment that is a positive one.

After spending a great deal of time around foals, I believe that when our children are born, they are perfect. Aside from genetic predisposition, they know very little fear, they are not judgmental, they are ignorant to race and gender differences, and they love us without reservation. In teaching them what they need to know in life, unfortunately, we also teach them prejudice, foolish pride, fear, and every other emotion that makes us more human but less perfect. I knew a mare that was otherwise perfectly acceptable; however, she pinned her ears every time someone approached. In the horse world, this is considered aggressive behavior. She never followed through with her threat, but she came to learn that it frightened people, so she continued to pin her ears. When this mare gave birth, she proceeded to teach her foal to do the same through example. The baby wasn't born knowing to do this because it wasn't genetic; however, as he spent more and more time with his mother, he learned by example.

Keys of Communication

There is really no great mystery in trying to better understand the people we meet and how to deal with the challenges we face in our lives. It is available to everyone who chooses to use it. It's a simple thing called common sense. If you trust your instincts and use your common sense in facing any challenge, you will have the key that unlocks the door to a good relationship with almost every person you meet and every challenge you face.

At no time in this book will I refer to any situation with a horse as a *problem*. Instead, we must think of it in terms of a lack of communication. Always approach the situation as a challenge rather than as a problem. This frame of mind is of the utmost importance. I am also not arrogant enough to claim to "own" another living creature. We are all God's creatures and we are equal in the overall scheme of things.

If you are not experienced enough to make a decision on your own, never hesitate to ask for help. I have had the privilege of knowing and loving horses for most of my life and I feel it would be safe to say that I have met hundreds, if not thousands, of horses. I have traveled around the country speaking with other horse people on a variety of horse-related subjects. Horses have taught me everything from how to better enjoy the best times in my life to how to survive during the darkest times. In writing this, my family has discussed at great lengths which stories have a lesson to teach and which horses have offered us the greatest challenges. In sharing these stories, we offer you insight into what we have discovered about our horses and ourselves, and we offer them to you as tools to use in your life.

With each new encounter, we have laughed not only at some of the horses and the stories they gave us, but also at ourselves. We have experienced the remarkable feeling of success as well as the unbearable grief that comes with saying goodbye. We have made our fair share of mistakes and have also dealt with the mistakes of those who had touched our horses' lives before us.

When we introduce ourselves to new horses, we immediately accept that each of them will have an entirely different personality. Their likes and dislikes, their fears, what they find enjoyable, and the limits to which you can safely push them all vary from horse to horse, just as they do with people. Some horses have the quiet yet intense mind of a poet; others have the fun-loving, entertaining personality of a clown. Once we take the time to discover a horse's individual personality, we can then use the tools of communication to better understand them and to apply those same principles to our everyday lives.

Your love of horses has brought you to this wonderful place and time in your life, so enjoy learning how you can apply what they teach you to your own life. Whether you share your life with a horse or have never had that experience, you will learn something new because this book is a study of human nature through observing animal behavior. It is my pleasure to introduce you to some of the most amazing horses I have had the privilege of knowing and loving and learning from over the last forty or so years. May these stories enrich your life and your relationships and help you to face challenges with hope and faith and, most of all, love.

Chapter One
Dewey

Experience Is the Best Teacher

$\mathcal{L}$ooking back, I suppose I had a strange childhood, but maybe it wasn't that different from most. We moved around a lot. We never left Ohio and Michigan, but we rented a lot of apartments and houses and changed schools usually about once or twice a year. Those were extremely difficult financial days for a family with six children. We got settled, but then we got evicted or made an attempt to get a nicer apartment, and we would move again. Dad did his best working various jobs, but trying to raise six kids (two boys and four girls, with ages ranging from 4 to 15) must have been quite a challenge. And keeping track of us? Forget about it! We were wild kids from the get-go. Mom had just graduated from trade school as a beautician, and our first house in the city was a cute little one that I remember only vaguely because I was only 6 years old at the time.

But the beauty shop—Katy's House of Kurls! It was attached to the front of our house, and it was our playground. We rented the actual house and attached space for the salon, but Mom, along with some fellow beauticians, opened the business. We caught frogs and put them in the formaldehyde solution that "the girls," which was how they referred to themselves, used to clean the combs and brushes. We laughed hysterically when one of the girls would open the unit for a brush or comb and scream at finding a frog instead. We begged sodas and chips from the customers; we would spin for long periods of time in the chairs and make faces in the mirrors. At Christmas time, the customers would bring presents of fudge and cookies and brownies and candy, and we would eat ourselves into comas.

Dad's best friends, aside from Mom's out-of-control brothers, were two men who worked at the gas station next door. Their names were "Gums" and "the one-armed man." Oh, I am sure they had real names, but I had no idea what they were.

My family used to spend Sunday nights gathered around the television to watch *Bonanza* and dream of having horses. Dad tells me now that Gums used to have a horse back then that he kept up at a riding stable in Michigan called Douglas Meadows. Every weekend, Gums would pack a bunch of beers in his saddle bags, ride all day while he drank, and eventually pass out on his horse. Dad tells me that the horse would then take him back to the stable, where the stable hands would put his horse away and let Gums sleep it off. To me, Gums was just a man with no teeth who drank a lot, but had I known he had a horse, I would have thought he hung the moon!

Dad used to sneak off with Gums and head up to Douglas Meadows to ride. My dad loved horses even back then. I loved the old westerns and used to say that when I grew up, I was going to have six boys and live on a ranch with a lot of horses. I had a photo of Roy Rogers and his horse, Trigger, that my dad had given me. It was my most treasured possession. I used to drive him nuts with the endless questions such as "What was Trigger called again, a Palomino?" and "How much do horses cost?" and "What was that thing that they tied to keep the saddle on?" I used to wear my brother's holster with the pearl-handled guns and pretend I was in a showdown at the O.K. Corral. There was just something about little girls and anything horses that seemed almost magical and still does today. I think it is universal.

One Sunday night—Palm Sunday, 1964, to be exact—we had all gone to bed after watching *Bonanza* and awoke to the sound of the tornado sirens blaring. My brother pushed me down the stairs and told me to go to the basement, but of course I froze in the middle of the living room in front of the big picture window because, suddenly, my ears felt like they were closing, and I heard a train. We didn't live near tracks at the time and the next thing I heard was my mother screaming, and then glass breaking. She was screaming because she was carrying my younger sister, and the attic door had come off and came down the steps and hit them. Mom saw blood and thought it was my sister bleeding but it was Mom's arm. The glass breaking was the picture window, the large plate glass one just in front of us, and I remember thinking how strange it was that the glass shattered in on us instead of blowing out.

Just as quickly as the tornado came, it was suddenly quiet again. Everything was ruined. The news crews came to the area and took footage, and neighbors helped neighbors. As we rummaged through our things, I found my photo of Trigger, wet and ruined. I was devastated. It taught me for the first time that life can be good, and then, in an instant, everything you worked for can be taken away. No one was hurt, but it was the first really bad thing that ever happened in my life. Jobs come and go, money was never ours to enjoy, but as a 7-year-old kid, devastation came down to that wet, torn photo of Trigger and Roy and the nightmares that followed that horrible night.

One Sunday, Dad told us we were going on a drive. This was his way of offering us something special in our lives without admitting that we didn't really have the money to do much else. We usually went to my grandparents house in Michigan or my Aunt Patsy's, but this time, we would do something so special that it would change my life forever. In the midst of all the chaos and the worry and the nightmares, we arrived at a place that was nothing short of the Emerald City in *The Wizard of Oz*. Douglas Meadows was like heaven to me. As we drove down the dirt road to the big barns, there were people on horseback! Not characters on a television show, but real people and real horses. They had saddles and bridles and western hats, and the horses smelled so good! I stuck my head out the window and could hear the horses nicker and call to each other, and I knew at that moment that I wanted to grow up and live on a ranch just like that one.

A really nice woman wearing red cowboy boots met us at the car. I don't remember her name, but I will never forget those red boots! Keep in mind that we were not at all savvy to the rules of a ranch, and we piled out of that car like the wild bunch of city kids we were. We didn't have red boots; we were barefoot and filthy and running around like a bunch of kids in a candy store. We had never seen horses before, and now here we were surrounded by nothing but horses. Mom and Dad thanked the nice woman, who led us past the fancy people on the pretty horses to a large paddock. There in the paddock, standing all by himself, was a tall, white horse. He was the oldest, sorriest excuse for a horse that anyone had ever seen, but I can honestly tell you that he was the most beautiful thing I had ever laid eyes on. I cried at his beauty, because to a little girl who had lost so much, Dewey represented everything I had ever wanted in life. He had four legs, a mane, and a tail and beyond that, I couldn't have cared less—he was a *horse!*

As I approached, I noticed his eyes were blue, not clear blue or bright blue, but dead blue. The horse was blind in both eyes. He stood there perfectly still as we climbed all over him and squealed with delight. He didn't spook at all, as though he understood our excitement and our lack of experience. The woman said that Dewey was almost 30 years old and had taken care of a lot of children while they learned how to ride, herself included. She hooked a lead rope to his halter and had my dad pile four or five of us on his back. We were all very little, and Dewey didn't mind at all. She walked us around, and then once in a while, she got Dewey to trot for a stride or two as we screamed and howled. Then she let each of us have a turn by ourselves.

Dewey knew his boundaries within the confines of the paddock, and he gave me a gift that day that I will not forget for the rest of my life. It was a feeling of freedom that I had not known until that moment; the freedom of thinking about something joyful during a very frightening time in my life. When I kicked and clucked to him as the woman instructed, I held on tight and he cantered! For the first time in my life, I didn't feel like one of six poor kids from the city. I was riding a horse for the first time, and I was in heaven. This broken-down, blind, old horse made a little girl's dream come true that day, and he taught me that all things are possible; that although bad things happen, good things happen, too; and that I was a survivor. From this one horse, the first of many that I would have the privilege to know and love and learn from, came a lifetime of discovery that would begin on that day.

I still get excited every time I see a pair of red cowboy boots or an old photo of Roy and Trigger. Dewey was old, but his years of experience gave me that moment, and to this day, I smile when I think of him. I still associate freedom and joy with riding a horse, with the wind in my hair, and with my troubles behind me.

Chapter Two
Red

Living Your Dream

*E*veryone has a dream; something you would truly love to achieve or acquire. Even if it is something that may seem absolutely unattainable, it is your dream nonetheless. Our dreams are what keep us going and are the spark of something better when all else seems lost. Dreams are what get us through the difficult times in our lives. In so many ways, our dreams are what keep us sane; they give us purpose in our lives and give us the strength to overcome every obstacle or challenge.

For as long as I could remember, my dad's dream was to have a horse of his own. He longed to live in the country, wake every morning, look out his window, and see a horse out in a vast green pasture of clover. It was one of the few things that my dad and I had in common. The reality of our financial situation was the biggest obstacle standing in his way. It seemed that he would get to a point in his life where he was so close to his dream that he could almost reach out and touch it, and then something would come along and yank it away.

My brother Joe was a very sick child from the time he was born. The doctors said that he would not make it through the first twenty-four hours of his life, and when he did, they said that he would not see his first birthday. When I came along, five years after Joe, he was still alive. Joe did not grow at a normal rate for a child of his age, and there were surgeries and hospital stays that accompanied his disabilities. With each setback he experienced came medical bills that eventually made my father's dream of affording a horse drift further and further away. He never gave up on Joe—and he never gave up on his dream.

I believe that the dream my father had was not as much for him as it was for all of us. It was the dream of knowing a better way of life. He worked two jobs, and Mom worked as well, and I watched as they struggled to get out of bed each morning to make sure that there was food on the table and a roof over our heads.

Babysitters came and went. They would hire a new one, and we kids (there were six of us) would proceed to chase her off with whatever torture we could devise on any particular day. On most days, my parents would leave for work, and we would just disappear. It was the late 1960s, and we lived in the inner city of Toledo, Ohio. Down the block was a soda pop manufacturer and next door to that, a potato chip factory. In the basement of the home in which we lived at the time, there was a hole in one of the walls that was large enough to hold several cases of pop that we had acquired from our neighbor and friend, the loading dock manager, and hundreds of bags of slightly outdated potato chips that they would give us. The six of us would haul chips and soda from the factories and hide them in the wall. We would pile various items in front of the hole so that no one would know that it was there.

One day, Miss Josie, our babysitter (or should I say, "our victim") at the time, walked out on the job and left us to fend for ourselves after someone mysteriously locked her in the closet. After she left, my oldest brother, Bill, and I pulled the mattress from one of our beds and placed it on the front porch just outside a broken window. We tied towels around our necks as capes and ran and dove through the opening where the glass had once been, landing on the mattress. Meanwhile, my brother Joe and my sisters made a slip-and-slide out of an old plastic tarp and powdered laundry soap.

My parents arrived home to complete chaos. I had missed the opening during one of my flying expeditions and had gone through the window next to the opening. My forearm had a piece of broken glass embedded in it, a cut that required fourteen stitches. My brothers and sisters had left the hose running for hours, and the yard was flooded. They were covered head to toe in blisters from the powdered soap they had used for the slip-and-slide.

The babysitter was never seen again, and all of us kids were pretty wired from the soda and chips that we had consumed all day. Dad took me to the hospital, while Mom hosed off the rest of the kids and put salve on their numerous sores. Because the water had flooded the neighbor's yard as well, she made a call, and our landlord showed up during all the commotion. He and my dad walked through the house while we waited on the front porch. We could hear their raised voices as they discussed various "problems" with the condition of the house. They found our stash of goodies in the wall and in his frustration, my dad said those words that had by now become no great surprise to us. He lined us all up, looked at us with absolute disgust and exhaustion, and quietly announced "We're moving."

We had moved at least two other times over the course of the following year, Joe had undergone at least two more surgeries, and we were all getting into trouble on a regular basis. The children in the new neighborhood would tease Joe for being so small and wearing a brace on his back, and Bill would beat them up. Eventually, he began lying and stealing, and his escapades steadily grew worse until the police became involved. Mom and Dad were still working. One day, my dad's friend Gums told him about a house in Swanton, a suburb of Toledo, that was for rent for very cheap. Gums also told him of a big red horse that was for sale at Douglas Meadows, a riding stable in Michigan. The owner of the horse was in some financial trouble and had to sell him.

Dad came home one day and announced that he had bought a horse and we were moving to a house in the country. The horse, Red, was a seventeen-hand Thoroughbred/Tennessee Walker cross, and we had yet to see him. Dad had worked odd jobs and cleaned stalls at another farm, saving every spare dime he earned, until he had exactly $150, a fortune back then. The price included all the items that he would need for a horse, including an old saddle and a box of brushes and combs.

When we first arrived, my sisters and I played inside the near empty truck that sat in the new driveway of our new house in our new town. The only differences between this house and the several others in which we had lived was the fact that it wasn't an apartment, we weren't guests at a relative's house, and it wasn't in the heart of the city. My mom hollered from the house and, as usual, the four of us ran as fast as we could in the opposite direction. Dad managed to catch my two brothers and drag them kicking and screaming into the house to help my mom unpack. I was 8 or 9 at the time with one sister two years younger, one sister two years older, and the other sister seven years older. My two brothers fell somewhere in between. It was June, and I was grateful that my parents waited until school was out before we moved "to the country" because it was always more difficult making new friends and leaving old ones behind while school was in session.

We had lived in three other houses in two years. "In the country" was what they called the location of this house, but as far as I was concerned, "in the middle of nowhere" was definitely more like it. The only shining light in this latest move was that we were getting a horse. My mind's eye pictured Dewey, the laid back blind horse with one foot in the grave and the easiest going manner that any horse could possibly possess.

Red could not have been further from what I expected. Dad had met two new friends, Rex Wiley, a cowboy from Texas, and Jack Osgerby, a man who lived across the street and had several horses. (Jack's wife, Carol, actually gave me my first pair of red boots. They were old and about three or four sizes too big, but I wore them anyway—I used to stuff toilet paper in the toes so they would stay on. I felt like the queen of everything in those boots.) Jack had the ability to calm any horse regardless of its disposition, and Rex had the ability to send my mother into a tirade every time he opened his mouth.

He cursed and he smoked and he drank too much, and he was the worst possible influence on us six kids that you could imagine. Of course, to me, he was from the West, a true cowboy, and much to my mother's dismay, I followed him everywhere he went. I imitated his swagger and his accent and everything about him. I learned a lot that summer: how to swear, how to spit, and how to find that one nerve that would send my mother into an absolute frenzy.

One of my most precious memories of Rex was what I refer to as "the dragonfly incident." In the meadow behind our house were hundreds of dragonflies. They would hover overhead and, at times, swoop down for bugs that were flying near us. They frightened me, so I asked my mother about them. She was having a bad day and was trying to get the laundry off the line because a storm was approaching. I don't think she realized how much they frightened me, and in her attempt to be funny, she told me that if I let them get too close, they would swoop down and sew my eyes and mouth shut. I shrugged off her words of wisdom with my usual defiant attitude and went off to play, but the thought of what she had said scared the heck out of me.

That night, as the sky darkened, I saw my big tiger cat run into the meadow. I wanted to catch him and bring him in the house before the storm hit, so I went after him. The wind picked up, and the clouds began to thunder. There I was, sitting in the middle of the meadow, paralyzed with fear. I could hear my mom call for me from the house, but I couldn't move. With the flashes of lightning came mental flashes of the night of the tornado and the shattering glass. Overhead, the dragonflies continued to circle and swoop, and I covered my eyes and my mouth so they couldn't sew them shut. I was sobbing so hard as they swooped down, and one of them actually brushed against my hair.

I sat there convincing myself that they were going to sew my eyes and mouth shut and that I wouldn't be able to breathe or see, and then the storm was going to spawn a tornado that would carry me away. Just as the rain began to fall and the dragonflies flew for cover, I heard someone approaching. It was Rex Wiley. He picked me up and carried me to the barn, which was the closest shelter from the storm. Once there, he hollered to the house that he had found me and I was fine.

He asked me why I was crying. I cried so hard as I told him about the tornado and the dragonflies and how they would sew my eyes and mouth shut if I allowed them to get too close. He looked angry as I recounted my mother's story to him. He told me that the Indians believed that dragonflies were spiritual guides that watch over you and protect you during difficult times and that they would not ever do anything to harm me in any way. I believed him, and as he explained this to me, the storm passed. There was no tornado, just a summer storm that quickly passed by. There was no longer any danger in playing in the meadow as the dragonflies hovered and swooped down for their dinner of mosquitoes and gnats. There was no fear because I felt safe again.

Rex, Jack, and my dad went to pick up Red, our new horse. As we waited for the trailer to arrive with Red, we argued over who would get to ride him first. When the three men pulled into the driveway in Jack's red truck and trailer, I discovered for the first time that just as with people, all horses are not alike. Red banged so loudly in the back of the trailer that I was sure that he was going to tip it over. The three men backed the trailer up to the gate of our pasture and swung open the door. That horse bolted through that door like a bullet out of a gun. He was sweaty from head to toe, and his nostrils flared as he pranced along the fence line in all his beauty. When we squealed and ran toward him in our excitement, he responded by striking the ground with his front hoof and calling loudly to any other horse within earshot. Across the street, Jack's horses called back, making Red more and more anxious. Horses are herd animals and do not like to be by themselves, and this was evident to me by his behavior.

Even through all the commotion that followed, as we were warned not to get too close until he settled in, I can still remember the look on my father's face. He was living his dream; he had a horse. Red did eventually settle down somewhat, but he was so incredibly different than Dewey, the easygoing old horse I'd ridden at Douglas Meadows. My curiosity grew as the three men worked with Red during those first few days he was home. I would sit on a fence rail and watch as they tried to saddle him and get him to allow them to put a bit in his mouth. I would absolutely drive them crazy with all my questions, and yet they would answer them patiently. Whether they realized it or not, they were giving me the tools that I would need to someday live my own dream.

Red continued to strike at them, and Rex knew how badly my brothers and sisters and I wanted to ride him, so one day, they decided to *lay him down.* This was a technique that was used quite a bit out west, and it worked most of the time. The idea was to lay the horse down, forcing him into total submission until he allowed the men to literally touch him all over and convince him that he had nothing to fear from them. It would be the first time that I realized I could actually feel the horse's fear and insecurity simply through the compassion I had for horses in general. With Dewey, you asked and he complied, but with Red, a different approach would be necessary if they were to get him beyond the point to which he had somehow gotten.

It was all done very quietly, with Rex taking the lead. The men put two ropes around Red's neck, and my dad held one in front and off to the left while Jack held the other opposite where my dad stood. Rex slowly lifted the horse's front hoof and held it there, while Jack moved in from the other side and leaned into the horse to carefully take him off balance. Red struggled at first as tears burned my eyes, but eventually, he lay down. Once on the ground, Rex knelt on the horse's neck while my dad approached him and began to talk to him, soothing him by rubbing his neck and touching his ears and his face and gradually working his way down the length of the entire horse.

This continued until Red was calm and did not fight their touch. I watched his eyes as they slowly relaxed and his breathing slowed and the men allowed the horse to stand. He didn't fight to stand but rather stood slowly and calmly, and then he shook off the dust and stood there as quietly as Dewey had. My dad removed the ropes from around his neck, placed a bridle over his ears, and offered him the bit. Red took it. Once the bridle was in place, they saddled the horse and walked him around the pasture. I wondered at this point whether laying him down had somehow stolen his beautiful spirit, but as my dad climbed up on his back, Red took exactly three steps and bolted through the pasture bucking. Nope, his spirit was still intact! My dad's pride was a bit wounded, I am sure. However, Red pranced through the pasture as if to say that although he now trusted the men more, he was still the same horse.

Dad dismounted and stood in the middle of the pasture until Red finally walked over to him and stood there. Dad's dream was a reality, and because he had worked so hard over the years to make his dream come true, I think he appreciated it even more.

I took the lessons I'd learned from Dad to heart: Put food on the table and a roof over your head. Work hard and take good care of yourself and your family, but never, under any circumstances, let go of your dream. It is what will keep you going when times get hard, and it will sustain you even through the most difficult challenges in your life. It will be your hope when all other hope seems lost, and with determination and conviction, someday you will achieve it if you believe it.

In the year and a half that followed, my dad, Rex, and Jack became very good friends. They would meet on Saturday mornings and ride down the road through the park for hours. Eventually, we all rode Red. I had recaptured that wonderful feeling of riding hard and fast through the fields around our house, bareback. (I was too little to lift the saddle, so I learned to ride without it.) My older sister was afraid of horses, so my younger sister, Chris, and I used to lure her out in the field with a story about baby bunnies or whatever we thought my work on any particular day. Once she was out there, we would chase her back home riding double on the horse. She would scream and cry and run to tell Mom, but by the time she reached the house, we would be gone. It was a fun summer, and I apologize to her because she is still deathly afraid of horses to this day. Even Joe would get a turn to ride Red on a good day when he was feeling up to it. I believe that it gave him a freedom that he would not otherwise have known. Everything was going great until that inevitable day arrived, and we heard the words we never looked forward to: "We're moving."

Chapter Three
Hollywood

Missed Opportunities

*T*hrough my dad's dream of having a horse, six children came to understand the pleasure of the country life and the joy of horses. But that dream was short-lived, and soon Dad was offered a really good job that offered health insurance and, for the first time in his life, job security. The position was with the Chrysler Corporation, and it was a union job, so it paid more money than he had ever seen in his life. We sold Red to a family friend and moved to Perrysburg, Ohio, where we rented a house on Front Street overlooking the river. The first thing we did was to seek out the nearest horses, and we found them rather quickly. Mr. Metcalf, who lived in the next town, had horses, but he also had throat cancer so he couldn't spend very much time in the barn with them. He was a wonderful man who allowed us to ride the horses and learn from him in exchange for our grooming the horses, cleaning their stalls, and doing all the other various chores that were required. My sister Chris actually bought a pony from him named Tobi with her babysitting money, but she eventually sold him. Loving a horse and actually being 100 percent responsible for a horse are two entirely different matters.

Every day in the summer, we would walk or hitch a ride out to Mr. Metcalf's barn, which was just short of five miles away from our house. We would turn the horses out, clean the stalls, ride for a bit, and then leave so that we could be home in time to do our chores before my parents got home from work. The kids from Mr. Metcalf's neighborhood became our best friends and although she was only 12 when she first met him, my older sister eventually married one of the boys who lived near the barn. They have been married for over thirty years now.

We had lived in Perrysburg for about two years when my dad lined us up once again and said those now-infamous words: "We're moving." We panicked, until he announced that he and my mother had finally gotten to a place in their lives where all of their hard work had paid off. They were buying a house! Not renting, but actually buying their first house. We would never have to make friends, only to move as soon as we settled in. It would be ours to keep. The best part of the news was that our new house was just over the bridge in the next town and closer to Mr. Metcalf.

We moved to Maumee and continued to go out to Mr. Metcalf's barn for a few years after that. Dad lost touch with his friend Jack Osgerby, and Rex Wiley moved back to Texas. Once high school came, I found that I had less and less time to spend with the horses, and Mr. Metcalf eventually died. We all grew up and went our separate ways, and I married the love of my life.

Years later, I was at a horse show, and there was a man who looked vaguely familiar to me. As he approached, there seemed to be no recognition on his part at all. He smiled and made eye contact and passed me with the most beautiful Palomino I had ever seen short of Trigger. As he passed, that smile brought a wave of nostalgic reminiscence, and I was suddenly taken back in time. Before I even completely realized who he was, I turned around and found myself saying "Jack?"

"Jack Osgerby?" I said again, and he stopped. It had been so many years since I had seen him, and although his face was weathered from the years, his smile and the twinkle in his eyes remained unchanged. He looked more closely at me and I said my name (my maiden name, of course). He smiled and remembered me, one of six kids who had followed him around and asked him endless questions about horses years earlier.

We spoke briefly because he was getting ready to ride this beautiful Palomino horse he was leading. I watched from the rail as he entered the ring. I didn't recognize the horse at all, but it was love at first sight. I watched as Jack rode the horse with the excellence that recalled his skills as a horseman. With just a light touch, he had the horse spinning in circles so fast that his beautiful long white mane was standing straight out to the side, and then he would stop dead and spin the other way. Jack would lightly cue him to pick up a canter, and then slide to a complete stop and spin again. It was the most beautiful dance I had ever had the privilege to see; it literally took my breath away. After their performance, the crowd cheered, and Jack led the horse back to where I was standing.

"Aren't you going to introduce me to your friend?" I asked. He told me that the horse's name was Hollywood and, apparently, the two of them had done quite well together. Over the years, Jack had won world titles and had become quite well-known for his training and riding skills. I, on the other hand, was just getting back into horses after being away from them for many years. I was in the position that my dad had been in years ago; I had to concentrate on keeping food on the table and a roof over my family's head. Jack invited my husband and me out to his place to ride Hollywood and a few weeks after, we took him up on it.

Jack's house was a shrine to all of his many accomplishments, and I couldn't help but appreciate that I had the blessing of having him in my life when I was first learning about horses. He told me that Rex Wiley did indeed move back to Texas shortly after we sold Red, our first horse, and moved away; however, Rex had also accomplished quite a bit and was well-respected for his achievements with horses.

I knew that Hollywood was worth a lot of money, probably more money than I would ever see in my lifetime, but with every part of my being, I wanted that horse. My husband had not yet really learned the joy of horses or come to understand their worth. Jack saw my love for that horse, but he also saw that I understood that this day was just a chance to ride the perfect horse and nothing more.

One day, Jack called me out of the blue and asked me whether I wanted Hollywood. I laughed because he always did have such a great sense of humor. When he said he was serious, I told him that although I was saving for a horse of my own, I could never afford this horse. He asked me how much I had saved and I told him. Believe me when I say that it wasn't much at all. He offered me Hollywood for a price that was at least one-tenth of what the horse was worth; however, it was still 100 times more than I could afford. I would have moved heaven and earth to have the pleasure of riding that horse every day of my life, but we had bills to pay and were not ready and couldn't afford it for so many reasons. I tried to convince my husband, and in doing so, somehow convinced myself, that it was the opportunity of a lifetime and that I couldn't afford to pass it up. But in the end, I had to pass it up.

I had spent my childhood moving from place to place and making new friends, only to move again; my husband and I wanted more than that for our two daughters. We wanted to build a place in the country where they could wake up every morning knowing they were home and no one was going to yank the rug out from under them. They would be able to know the same friends from their childhood into adulthood. I didn't care how hard I had to work in order to give that to them. I believe that there is a path that we are supposed to take in order to get to where we are going, and buying Hollywood would definitely have been a detour. All sensible logic aside, I'd wanted that horse so badly. He was perfect, and he belonged to the man who had helped nurture my love for horses. I knew there would come a day when I would look back at that time as a missed opportunity; however, I didn't understand to what extent until I found out a short while later that Jack Osgerby was dying.

He eventually sold everything he owned, Hollywood included, and his life ended on January 17, 1998. I believe that he knew he was dying long before he told anyone. He didn't tell me; however, he offered to sell me that horse for pennies on the dollar. It was a missed opportunity that, on some level, I will regret for the rest of my life, but regardless, I am so incredibly grateful that Jack had touched my life again.

I believe that there is a path we are supposed to take in our lives. Call it destiny or fate or whatever you wish, but Hollywood taught me that if we dwell on the missed opportunities in our lives, we forget to be grateful for the opportunities we do have. We are all blessed with the freedom of choice, and whatever plays a part in the decisions we make, we have to move on and not dwell on what might have been. Years later, my husband would come to realize the value and importance of that horse and would also have some regret for our decision to pass on Hollywood. But along our chosen path, we have still had the privilege of meeting and knowing and loving so many horses, all of whom taught us so many important lessons.

Jack Osgerby will forever be among the few really important people in my life. May he rest in peace, and may Hollywood live a good many years. I never saw Hollywood again after he was sold, but I will remember him for the rest of my life.

Chapter Four
Clarissa

Relationships and Limitations

*P*eople will have expectations of you, and it is up to you to consider how far you are willing to extend yourself in order to please them. Relationships can be difficult, whether professional or personal.

My husband's name is Michael, but everyone has referred to him as "Bear" for years. When we first met, he didn't give horses a thought. His interests were in other areas. When we would go to people's houses, the kids and I would immediately go to the barn to meet the horses. Later, though, Bear would not even remember that there were horses there at all. He was even totally oblivious to the animal that is now an important part of his life.

Jennifer, our youngest daughter, has always been my horse person. She learned early how to ride and care for them, and she has accomplished quite a bit over the years. Dusty, our oldest daughter, has other interests, and, although she loved growing up in the country, she doesn't share the love of horses with her younger sister.

Bear and I paid our dues early on by living in the city and raising enough money to build a house in the country. Bear actually built a barn for me before we finished the house, because I came home one day and told him that I had bought a horse. His reply was, "That's nice," and he began building a small barn with a tiny tack room attached. He never even saw the horse until I brought her home weeks later.

Clarissa was a white Arabian mare who stood approximately fifteen hands tall. She had belonged to a friend of our older daughter, and the friend's mom agreed to sell her to me under one condition— if I ever decided to part with her, she would go back to their barn. Easy promise to keep, right? Not really. In fact, I don't suggest that you make this agreement with anyone. If you are going to purchase a horse or even if you are given one completely free of charge, do not let someone else control what it is that you will do with the horse. For that matter, this advice applies to any deal that you make with anyone on anything. When agreements come with conditions attached to them, they tend to become extremely complicated.

Mr. Metcalf was a generous man who had allowed us kids to ride his horses under the condition that we do the chores. However chores were something I loved to do almost as much as riding! We were excited to finally have a horse of our own. Bear, Dusty, and Jen would learn to ride on Clarissa, so she was the first horse for all of us.

Bear paid very little attention to Clarissa; that is, until he saw how much fun I was having with my horse friends. He had been on horses only two times when he was quite young, and both rides ended in disaster. On one ride, his horse had bolted and was running full-out in a field as the saddle slowly slipped under the horse. The cinch had not been tightened properly, and Bear had nearly been killed. Now that we had Clarissa, he wanted to experience the pleasure of having a good ride.

One day, after my friend Marty and I had returned from a ride, Bear asked whether he could ride Clarissa. I was surprised because, by this time, Clarissa had quite a reputation. When we first purchased her, we were told that she was a good trail horse and had been shown in 4-H. At times however, she could be a little high-strung. The problem didn't lie so much in what we were told but rather what we were *not* told. For example, we were not told that she had once reared at a show and sat down on a picnic table full of people. Other aspects of her reputation I had experienced firsthand. Clarissa would walk by an object for twenty-nine days in a row and show no concern over it, but alas, on the thirtieth day, it was suddenly a threat to her. She had cantered up to a mud puddle with every intention of jumping it, only to stop dead in her tracks and launch me over her head into the puddle. My daughter Jennifer had been on her, but only a few times and under strict supervision.

Fully aware of the horse's reputation, Bear took the reins anyway and took on the challenge. My friend Marty and I sat on the front porch as Bear got up on Clarissa in the side yard and came around the house to where we could see him. Just as he cleared the side of the house, I asked him whether he was all right. He smiled and assured me that he was. He spoke too soon, and his smile diminished as Clarissa reared up in the air and dumped him on the ground. I will never forget the look on his face for as long as I live: surprise; a touch of fear; and some genuine, old-fashioned anger.

Luckily, Bear grabbed the reins before Clarissa could bolt down the road. The road had become her favorite escape route after dumping a rider. Bear stood and brushed off the dirt. I figured he was finished, so I went to take the mare from him, but he stopped me. He was apparently ready for round two, and that is exactly what he got. He positioned himself in the saddle and asked her to move forward. She did her signature dance, a sideways prancing motion, and proceeded to throw him again. Round three took him to the road, where Clarissa spotted a yellow chalk line on the pavement, and off he came again. I was getting very worried, while my friend Marty was rolling on the ground, laughing at this determined new horse person who just refused to give up.

Eventually, Bear took Clarissa down the road and didn't come back for almost an hour. He later explained to us that she tried every trick in the book while they were together on their ride, and he took each challenge she offered and faced it with determination. Bear felt that if he gave up and walked away, she would win, and he would most likely never have wanted to ride again. Instead, he faced the challenge and learned a few lessons, even if he walked away a little scraped and bruised as a result. And for as long as we had her, she never challenged him to that level again.

This approach is not for everyone. Certainly, now that we have more experience, both of us can see a million things we would have handled differently with Clarissa, but we were new horse owners, and the lessons she taught us were so valuable. Safety of horse and rider should never be compromised. However, getting on a horse after you have been thrown is facing a fear and accepting a challenge. This is why we do not refer to a horse's shortcomings as "problems," but rather as "challenges;" another similarity to people. The question to ask yourself in a situation such as this is whether or not you're up to the challenge. It has to be a personal decision. If at any point in a relationship with anyone, you feel it is a challenge you don't want to deal with—or that you cannot deal with—do both yourself and the other person a favor and walk away.

Not only did Bear find that he was up to the challenge that day, but he also found something much more important. He found his love of horses—a love that would take him on a journey that would change him forever. Clarissa gave Bear the tools of communication that he would use for years to come. He didn't know it at the time, but those lessons of determination and perseverance he learned on Clarissa would literally save his life one day.

Clarissa also taught Jen several very good lessons, helping her to understand the intelligence and uniqueness of her particular personality. Jen eventually went to work at an Arabian ranch and even handled the owner's Arabian stallion. Jen also learned to deal with difficult people both in her professional and personal life.

The lesson Clarissa taught me is one I will never forget. She hated water with a passion. Bath time always proved to be a challenge with her. She would watch as I got out the hose, the shampoo, and all the other items I needed to wash her, and she would nervously prance along the fence line in her corral in trepidation of what lay ahead. One day, Jen had some friends over, and they were swimming in the pool. It was incredibly hot, and I decided to give Clarissa a bath. She was more anxious than usual with the sound of the screaming kids and the splashing of the water. I didn't have a wash rack or a hitching post at the time, so I did something that I see now as incredibly stupid on my part. It pains me to even admit it, but it was another lesson learned. I threw the lead rope over the top of a twelve-foot metal gate, trying to give her the illusion of being tied. She tied well, so I assumed she would stand there and let me bathe her. The lead rope had a knot in the end of it that we used to prevent the lead from slipping through our hands when she would attempt to run off.

I was wearing a bathing suit, so that I would be cool, and my cowboy boots, so that my feet would be protected. Clarissa stood rather quietly while I sprayed her off and soaped her up. Everything was going well until I stepped in front of her to wash her chest. This put me between her and the metal gate. I turned on the sprayer once again, just as one of the kids did a cannonball into the pool. Clarissa spooked and backed up. When she did this, the knot in the end of the lead rope got stuck in the panels of the metal gate. It ripped the gate right off of its hinges, knocked me over, and scraped it against my bare back. I gasped as I watched a soapy lathered horse run into the woods with a twelve-foot gate hanging from the end of a lead rope. I remember thinking to myself in the split second before she hit the trees that, for the first time since I had known her, she hadn't run down the road. She bolted through the woods, the gate clanging on her legs, and through the passing branches I could no longer see her.

I got up and ran after her. At about the halfway point to the back of the woods, I found her running full-out, with the gate still banging behind her. The gate hit two trees and wedged between them, stopping her in her tracks. She wriggled, broke free, and kept running. I arrived where the gate lay, and it was covered in blood. I knew she was hurt, and all I could think of was getting to her and calming her down. I kept running after her, my own wet body covered in dirt. Clarissa turned and ran right toward me. I cried as I saw her. She didn't even look like the same horse that had disappeared into the woods. Through the blood and the dirt, you could barely tell that she was a white horse.

She ran past me, her eyes wild and filled with fear. Clarissa ran toward one of Jen's friends who was perched in a tree, and the frightened girl screamed. This scared the horse even more, and she suddenly remembered that her safe place was the road. I ran, too—through the yard, out the front, and down the road after her.

The neighbor heard the commotion and saw me running after the horse in my bikini and red cowboy boots; both of us covered in dirt and blood. She came after me in her car and I immediately jumped on the front hood. Clarissa kept running, and we watched as she ran through an intersection and was almost stuck by a passing car. I was in this predicament all because I threw a lead rope over a gate. It truly seemed like a perfectly harmless thing to do at the time.

I was in pretty good shape at the time, but out of total fear, I still thought my heart was going to give out on me. I was so afraid that this horse would die due to my own stupidity that all I could do was cry. Then I saw a man, a neighbor that I had never met, mowing his grass on a small tractor. I whistled and he looked down the road toward what was surely the strangest sight he had ever seen in his quiet little neighborhood. A bloody, dirty horse running down the road with a crazy woman in a bikini and cowboy boots on the hood of a car, crying, "Catch my horse!" He ran out and put his hands up in front of the horse and she stopped, reared up and headed for his barn. We were able to corral her in one of his stalls. This is how I met our neighbor, Jack. I thank God that he was there that day. As we talked, we realized that we had known each other years ago when I was about 12 years old. Jack had been a friend of the family, and now we were neighbors and hadn't even realized it.

We called the vet and he came over and stitched Clarissa up and tended to all of her wounds, which were really not all that bad under the circumstances. She did, however, have to stay at Jack's barn for a few days until she calmed down enough for me to take her home.

I can remember going over to Jack's barn and sitting alone and sobbing. My stupidity had caused harm to an innocent animal. I realized at that point how important it was to really understand each and every horse—and each and every person—who comes into our lives. Every one of their likes, dislikes, and fears will determine the limit to which you can safely take them. Clarissa was never an incredibly lovable horse; in fact, she never appreciated attention at all. Her only goal was to get away from people as fast as she could.

To this day, I have yet to forgive myself for putting another living creature in harm's way, and I will forever remember that day. I still have nightmares about it. I take full responsibility for all that happened where this horse was concerned. The biggest lesson my family and I learned was to be sure that you have the temperament, patience, and experience to deal with specific personalities in life, because they may challenge you beyond your limits.

Clarissa stayed with us for a few more months before we decided she was not the right horse for us. I called the woman who had owned her and asked her if she wanted Clarissa back. She laughed at me and told me that she didn't. We listed her in the local paper. We had several people call about her, and we were completely honest about the fact that we felt she was not suitable for beginners. One of the inquiries was from a man who sounded experienced enough to handle her antics. He came to see her and seemed to get along with her great, so he bought her.

The next day, the woman who'd owned her originally called us, upset because we had sold her. She didn't want the horse back; she wanted us to keep her! That, in my opinion, was not her decision to make. She felt that it was. Consequently, we parted ways and have never spoken since.

Clarissa showed us where our limitations were. She taught us that personalities vary greatly and sometimes clash. Relationships can be extremely difficult sometimes, and you must set limitations or boundaries on what you are willing to do to keep the relationship strong. Know your own limitations and know that your personality will not always mesh well with another.

Chapter Five
Bart

Trusting Your Instincts

*I*nstinct is a pretty amazing thing to possess. We all have some instinctual ability; however, I have found that some of us are blessed with more than others. It is when we *don't* listen to our instinct that we sometimes get into trouble. If we set all logic and reason aside for a moment and consider that basic gut feeling that we sometimes experience, we understand instinct.

When it is time to consider whether we should buy a horse, I am usually with my husband, Bear, and my youngest daughter, Jennifer. Whether or not we actually bring the horse home is decided by a vote. Since there are three of us there, two of us have to agree that the horse is going to be loaded into the trailer, or we leave. This usually goes pretty well; however, on one particular occasion, Jennifer and I both agreed to pass on the horse, but Bear did everything in his power to convince us otherwise.

Oral reasoning is a sensible approach when judging horses. Normally, the reasoning covers points such as the horse's overall conformation, way of going (a horse's ability to move correctly), and structural soundness. However, when you're standing with an old horse trader holding registration papers that don't even come close to matching the horse—whose name was Bart—oral reasoning simply goes out the window. When the man who is trying to sell you the horse is saying things such as, "Y'all could throw a kid up on that horse," and yet refuses to ride the horse himself, red flags tend to go up.

Jen and I noticed scars from several previous injuries, and the condition of Bart's teeth told us Bart was definitely older than the 6 years on his registration papers. Bear saw only a horse that had a sweet disposition and a kind eye, while we were seeing papers that said this gelding was actually a mare, because the registration papers that the man was offering were not the papers for this particular horse. If the decision were left to Bear, bless his heart, we would get every horse he met because he is sure that it is just meant to be. Bear was just discovering that there was a little more to buying a horse than the desire to bring them all home.

Jennifer distracted the man while I got a second or two to let Bear in on what she and I were seeing, and we said goodbye to Bart. Some people we knew purchased him shortly after our visit. Two days after they paid cash and brought the horse home, Bart came up severely lame. He ended up at the auction because he couldn't be ridden at all. (When I say "the auction," I refer to it in the sense that it is most often the place where an owner takes a horse who is too unsuitable to sell. Auctions in general can be a very good place to purchase a horse; however, the one I'm speaking of was not.)

We have seen people tranquilize horses before selling them so that they will behave for the potential buyer. What is worse is that these people have no remorse when someone gets seriously hurt once the drugs wear off the horse; at least, they don't have enough remorse to prevent them from doing it again. We have met horses who had developed ringbone, founder, or navicular, and the seller gave them drugs to mask the pain until the seller made the sale. Don't get me wrong, there are some wonderful and honest people in the horse world, but there are also some that I would like to literally tattoo with a sign on their forehead that reads, "I am an idiot and a thief! Do not buy a horse from me!" It would make life so much easier for new horse people who have decided to buy their first horse.

Two lessons could be learned from Bart and his owner. One is that when you go to look at a horse, take an experienced horse person with you, one who can see beyond the initial sales technique of the seller, because there are no morals with people such as Bart's owner. The other lesson is to always trust your instincts. If the seller tells you that something is just not what it seems, ask questions and base your decision on common sense.

As we got in the truck with our empty little red two-horse trailer behind us, Jennifer commented that, aside from all of the things that we'd noticed with Bart, she had a feeling from the moment we pulled into the driveway that we should not bring this horse home. Something told her that we should leave immediately and not even look at the horse. Bear laughed because he said he had the same feeling until he saw the beautiful gelding standing in the pasture, and his curiosity got the best of him. He put all other instincts aside and went to see the horse.

As we drove home that night, it was already dark, and we were approaching some railroad tracks that were on a pretty busy stretch of the road. Just as we hit the tracks, the trailer hitch broke, as did our safety chains. When we felt the bump, we looked back to see our trailer come completely unhitched from the truck. The tongue of the trailer shot sparks up from the pavement that could be seen for miles. The empty trailer came to a stop quickly. Had Bart been in the trailer, the weight would have surely shifted, and the trailer would have either gone into the oncoming traffic or rolled. I have only known one or two other people who have had this happen; each time, there was a horse in the trailer and the experience ended in disaster. I know that it may have been a coincidence that the trailer came unhooked from the truck, but the outcome was not any worse than it was because we followed our instinct. We were lucky that night because our trailer was empty and no one was hurt.

Horses have excellent survival instincts. They instinctively know when a predator is near or when trouble is ahead. We as human beings are given that same ability. The key is to listen to your instincts. You are going to meet people in the course of your life who send up red flags. If your instincts tell you to walk away, walk away! If you feel that something is just not right above all reason and logic, chances are your instincts are right and you should just move on.

Chapter Six
Baby

Trial and Error

*W*hen learning and growing as a person, you are going to try new things. In any challenge that you face in your life, you are going to try to overcome the situation through trial and error. You may fail in your attempt, but with perseverance, you will try another approach. This is how we grow as people and learn to better deal with the challenges that we face.

The horse bug had bitten my husband, Bear, pretty hard in that he had found his love for them. This man has always loved animals, having raised everything from armadillos and raccoons to snakes and opossums. You have no idea how many critters have paraded through our home.

Bear and I were renting a house in Stuart, Florida, back when we were both younger. I had just returned home after several days in Ohio. My brother Joe and I had driven twenty-three hours straight in a van with two dogs and a young child. Jennifer hadn't been born yet, and our other daughter, Dusty, was only 3. Joe and I were tired, and we arrived at the house to find Bear standing in the front yard with a young boy who was holding a cardboard box. He had heard that Bear adopted snakes, and he had one for him. We watched as Bear opened the box to expose the most beautiful snake I had ever seen. This particular one turned out to be a coral snake—one of the most dangerous snakes out there. I don't remember whether it is deadly, but it seems to me that if you didn't die, the experience would be painful enough that you would wish you had.

As I walked in the house after telling the boy that he would have to take the snake away immediately, it became obvious to me what Bear had been doing while I was gone. My home was now a zoo. There was an armadillo wandering aimlessly through the house; a laminated reptile hotel complete with lights and heaters housed snakes and lizards; a kitten with a bad cold was vomiting; an alligator—I'm not kidding, *an alligator*—was in the bathtub; and just outside the back door was a barrel with a mama opossum and her babies. Joe laughed as a newly acquired Labrador puppy got to fighting with his dogs and almost knocked over the fish tank. It was a madhouse! Just then, the landlord showed up from Canada for an unexpected visit. I was in tears. I tried desperately to keep him out front and not grant him admittance to "Bear's South Florida Zoo," all the while still dealing with the boy who wanted $10 for a poisonous snake. The night before, it had rained heavily, and Bear had shown up at work to find a cow that had gotten lost and ended up at the shop. The guys offered to help him get it to our house; thankfully, they didn't have a trailer large enough, or I would have been trying to hide a cow from our landlord. As it was, our lease specified "no pets."

This is how Bear is when it comes to animals of any kind. The man simply loves animals. So when he discovered his love of horses and wanted to devote more time to them, he gave up all of his other animals except the dogs and went to work learning absolutely everything he could about horses. He read every book and magazine he could get his hands on, and he spent hours either entertaining or alienating my horse friends with endless questions.

After Bear learned how important effective and consistent training was, he made it his goal to start a horse himself and see how great a horse he could create. We were both realizing the importance of genetics in a horse's ability to do specific tasks such as reining, cutting, pleasure riding, or jumping. We recognized the Thoroughbred influence in the Quarter Horse lines and how it had changed the look and performance of the breed, but more specifically we recognized how people have the ability to influence the growth of a breed through responsible breeding. We were huge fans of the old Foundation Quarter Horse bloodlines, due to their athletic ability and wonderful dispositions. I encouraged Bear to buy a 2-year-old Quarter Horse and start the training of a horse from scratch. We bought a little bay named Baby from some horse folks from Missouri.

Baby was a great project for Bear. There was very little that she was afraid of, and she was curious about everything. We started with groundwork and manners, and she was coming along nicely. We taught her the basics of her training, and Bear was learning right along with her, applying and experimenting with each new technique he read about. She did tend to rear on the longe line, twist, and get tangled up in the line, so we learned to maneuver the line better. We ground drove her and when we put the saddle on her for the first time, she stood there calmly. She was wonderful until it came to tying her. This mare could break any ties we put her in. She would feel the rope get tight, panic, and immediately free herself.

When I was young and used to watch those old westerns on television, it always amazed me that Gene Autry, John Wayne, and Roy Rogers could tie their horses to a hitching post for hours. They would go into the saloon, or have a gunfight, and when they came back, those horses would still be standing there. Not Baby. I don't think she ever watched those old westerns.

Bear made a hitching post for Baby one weekend. He set the 4x4s in concrete, and his last words were how there wasn't a horse alive who could break free from this sturdy new structure.

Monday morning, some friends and their children were coming over, and we decided to play with Baby, so we got her out and tied her to the hitching post. Between Carol and her husband, Paul; Marty and her husband, Tim; and Bear and me, we had seven children who ranged in age from 7 to 15. They were all girls. It was summer, and the children were usually with us all the time. These girls never sat still for more than five minutes all summer. While we were trying to get the tack out and get Baby ready for her ride, they were all running around and playing. One of the kids had tied eight or nine good solid knots in the lead rope that was attached to the hitching post—and attached to Baby. Just as we placed the saddle on her back, she jerked back and instead of breaking her halter or her lead rope, she broke the hitching post. On one side, it broke off at the top rail, and on the other side, it broke off about halfway down the post.

Here we were with a yard full of screaming girls and a 2-year-old horse with a hitching post hanging from her face. Well, needless to say, she didn't like the weight of it very much, so she staggered through the yard trying to shake it off. Every time she moved, the hitching post would throw her off balance, and she would stagger more. We got the girls on the porch and followed Baby around untying knots whenever she would stand still long enough for us to get close to her. Carol was finally able to get close enough to unstrap her halter and free her from the mess of the hitching post. We laughed when Bear came home from work and saw what was left of his wonderful new hitching post, the one he had sworn no horse could break.

Trial and error is definitely something to take into consideration. Along with the wonderful suggestions and advice we receive from people, we try different methods we have read about or theories we have developed through experience. If those don't work, we find and try something else.

Just after the incident with the first hitching post, a dear friend of ours named Henry Zumfelde helped us with Baby and her fear of being tied. If you ever have the opportunity to spend some time with a person from the *old school*—someone who has been there, done that, and lived to tell about it—I suggest you take the opportunity. You will not only get some wonderful tips on how to face your challenges but also hear some great stories.

Henry was 76 years old when he graciously volunteered to come over to our barn and teach Baby how to stand and behave while tied to a hitching post. When I picture Henry in my mind, I picture Jimmy Stewart: tall, very polite, and a great storyteller. Henry used to make buggies for Sauders Village, a wonderful old-town setting, where people can take tours and see what life was like in the old days. Henry taught the horses to pull the buggies. He had a very calm nature and loved horses as much as he loved people.

When Henry arrived, Carol, Marty, Bear, and I greeted him, while all of the girls ran around as usual. He introduced himself to Baby, immediately earning her trust by stroking her and talking to her. He was setting her mind at ease for what he was about to do. We had no idea how he was going to teach Baby to tie. We trusted his years of experience and his honest nature, and we were sure that at his age, he had trial and error down to a science. He took four lead ropes and tied two to each of the posts in the doorway of the little barn. If Baby did manage to get loose, she would not be able to go very far because the doorway connected to a fenced paddock. He put a second halter on her and proceeded to hook the lead ropes to the halters. She stood quietly until he reached up to fasten the last one. Baby backed up until the rope got taut, and she realized that she was tied.

Baby immediately tried to break free, knocking Henry against the wall of the barn and cutting his hand. Our instinct was to run to him, but he raised his hand and stopped us before we could get there. He calmed Baby and spoke to her softly. She remained quiet until he left her alone, and then she went crazy once more. He could see the fear in my eyes as I watched her struggle and listened to her bang herself against the walls of the barn. He knew that it was killing me to do nothing. He took his handkerchief from his pocket and wiped the blood from his hand.

Very casually, he asked me whether I would go to the house and make him some lemonade. I stood inside the back door of the house and cried, all the while fighting the urge to go back out and set Baby free. I thought about Clarissa and the fact that I had unintentionally hurt her. Now here I was taking part in hurting another horse. I couldn't stand it. I knew that I trusted Henry, but this was putting that trust to the test. I proceeded to make him some lemonade as he had requested. When I was finished, I dried my eyes and went back outside. I didn't want him to know how upset I was.

When I opened the back door to join the others, I was amazed by what I saw. Henry had tamed the wild girls. Baby was still thrashing and had broken two of the four lead ropes, but the girls—these kids who wouldn't sit still for more than five minutes—were circled around Henry. They were sitting on the ground in front of his lawn chair listening while he told them a story. I was truly impressed because we hadn't been able to get them to sit still at the same time for the entire summer. I handed Henry the glass of lemonade, and he smiled at me. His manner was still extremely calm and reserved. Immediately, I was assured that everything would be all right. I realized that this kind man knew exactly what he was doing.

Every so often, one of us would sneak a peek at Baby through the tack room door behind her where she couldn't see us. She was wet with sweat, but she was still fighting the ropes and struggling to break free. This went on for about another ten or fifteen minutes, and then everything went quiet in the barn. Henry continued to finish his story at his own pace, and then rose from the chair. He went in and spoke to Baby once more, and then released her, walking her out of the barn. She was wet with sweat and her legs were shaking, but other than a few scrapes on her face where she had struggled with the halter, she was fine. He handed her to Bear and asked him to walk her out a little bit.

I walked Henry to the car and half-jokingly asked him what he had said to her. He told me that horses were no different than people—they have to learn to trust you before you ask anything of them. He also explained to me that whenever we put our horses in a situation where they are fighting themselves, we accomplish more because they will not associate their frustrations with us. Lastly, Baby had to learn what we wanted from her—to stand quietly while tied.

Baby finally did learn that it was easier to stand quietly than to struggle. She learned this through her own trial and error. By panicking and breaking free from posts, she had reinforced her own fear that being tied was scary and that if she broke free, she would be okay. She would never associate any of us with the experience she had that day because we stayed away from her until she figured it out on her own. I didn't realize it until years later, but Henry knew that my fears for Baby were fueling her own and that as long as I was afraid, she would be, too. That was why he sent me to the house to make the lemonade. Both Baby and I had learned a very valuable lesson.

As Henry reached his car, he handed me the glass of lemonade that was still pretty full. I thanked him for what he had done, and he thanked me for the lemonade and left. I tasted it and realized that, in my anxiety over Baby thrashing in the barn, I had forgotten to put any sugar in it.

Baby never again refused to tie and although we saw Henry several times after that, he never again mentioned the incident—Baby or the lemonade. I know that by meeting and learning from Henry Zumfelde and others like him, I am a better person. I also know in my heart that by the horses we meet, we are better people as well, because they teach us so many things about ourselves, including how to deal with the challenges in our own lives.

We continued to work with Baby and learned so much from the experience. Horses made Bear act like a kid with a new toy—he couldn't get enough of them, and Baby was just the beginning. Although she was Bear's project, she was a learning experience for all of us. As with every horse with which we eventually part company, we still talk to her owners now and then. Baby turned out to be a great little horse. Thanks to her, we have a hitching post that is made of telephone poles secured safely in the ground with concrete.

Always be willing to try new things in your life, and if they don't work out for whatever reason, be willing to step up and try again. Always admit your errors and be grateful for them—they are just one of the many stepping stones that will lead you to every good thing that life has in store for you.

Chapter Seven
Harley and Star

Second Chances

I have always loved auctions, and one year, a friend of ours told us about a huge horse auction in a neighboring state the day after Thanksgiving. I didn't know what a horse auction was like at the time, but since neither my husband, Bear, nor I had to work that day, we decided to go.

When we arrived, the place was filled with people. There was such excitement in the air as we watched the horses being unloaded and brought into the huge barns. Bear and I couldn't wait to get a number and join in on the fun. His enthusiasm when it came to horses was indescribable. The man loved horses and just couldn't get enough. He walked around the grounds and spoke with everyone, asking questions and comparing techniques with each person he met. We were having such a wonderful day.

As we walked through the barns, we neared an area toward the back where very few people were standing. I stopped Bear, telling him that we should go the other way, as I was sure he didn't want to go back there. I had been warned about the *killer pens* that are packed with horses that, for one reason or another, are no longer useful to their owners. Some are just old or have cancer or broken legs, while others are simply deemed renegades and untrainable. Although we view our horses as friends and partners in work and play, the sad reality is that some other countries see them as food. There are people who buy these horses by the pound and sell them to other countries for meat. For lack of a better alternative than to bury each and every horse we have to put down, they go to these killer pens. Although I've pledged to give you an honest insight into each of the horses and what we have learned from them, I will spare you some of the more gruesome details of the killer pens.

As we approached the area at the back of the barn, I watched my husband's eyes, as I couldn't bring myself to look at first. I can tell you from his expression and from several conversations we would later have, that what he saw changed him in ways beyond what I can describe. Bear is the single most compassionate person I know. You wouldn't be able to tell this by first glance. He is a burly guy with a full beard and dark curly hair, but in those deep blue eyes of his, he bares his soul. He stood there for the longest time, completely void of any emotion other than pure, unadulterated grief. In the background, I could hear people laughing and having fun, as we had been doing just moments ago.

I followed Bear's eyes to a pen that was approximately twenty feet by sixty feet, in which the horses were so close together that they could barely move. Some were so thin that they had actually fallen down and were being walked on by other horses. Some were trying to get away from angry, more aggressive horses that were biting and kicking at them. There was barely any room for them to move out of the way. A few of them had large sores, and one actually had a broken leg that dangled from its shoulder. If you know about such places, you realize that they are rarely ever talked about. If you have never experienced such a place, I apologize for my honesty.

I looked back to where Bear had been standing, and he was no longer there. I looked around the crowded auction house to see where he had gone, when I saw that he was in the pen with the horses. I called to him to come out because I was so afraid that he would be hurt, but as he kept walking, I realized that he was heading for a horse toward the back that had its leg caught between the rails of the pen.

While Bear was making his way through the crowd of horses, a woman and her husband stopped to ask me what he was doing. I told them that he was going to help a horse that was caught before it broke its leg. She laughed and said, "Why bother? They are just killer pen horses; they're gonna die anyway." I couldn't believe her insensitivity to his kindness.

I am a very sympathetic person, as is Bear, and maybe after a while, some of us can become cold to the reality of these horses, but for as long as I live, it will still bother me terribly. We both truly love horses and find it difficult to understand how some people can be so heartless. We have worked with some pretty incredible horses over the years that other people refused to work with, and we were able to find some exceptional horses beneath the endless amounts of stupidity that their owners had instilled in them.

Bear and I were 4-H advisors at the time, and a young man we are proud to call our friend actually bought a horse from the killer pens at this auction. The mare was called Rory. She was deemed untrainable and sent there, where this young man bought her for next to nothing. He worked with her and the following year, he used her as a 4-H project. He qualified for the State Fair with this mare and placed in the top five there. He won literally everything he entered at the County Fair. This doesn't happen all the time, of course, and I wouldn't suggest that this is a good idea for just anyone, but it is sure nice to see that some of these horses do make it. Our friend gave Rory a second chance, and she delivered beautifully.

Bear and I also bought two horses at the auction that day. One was a little Palomino mare by the name of Star, and the other was a leopard Appaloosa named Harley. Our daughter Jennifer immediately fell in love with Star, but we found out days later that Star had been drugged to mask the pain of ringbone. We sold her to a ranch, where they used her as a companion horse and allowed her to be turned out to pasture. Harley, on the other hand, had by far the funniest personality we had ever met. We are taught all of our lives how to deal with the personalities of people, so when horse lovers meet a horse, they tend to ask themselves, "If he were a person, what would he be like?" This personal approach is extremely helpful in working through the challenges horses offer.

Harley was like a silly, playful child. He was curious about everything and looked at every task as a game. He would pick up buckets full of water and flip them over, and even pour the water on his own head. Then he would run and buck and toss his head. He was so entertaining. He loved people and saw us as new playmates. We rode him for a few months and taught him that there was a time to play and a time to be serious and pay attention. We eventually sold him to a family with a lot of kids, and he taught them to ride. They kept him for a couple of years, and then sold him to an English riding stable because they were ready to move on to a larger horse. He is used as a lesson horse now and gets to play with kids all day long.

As for the horses whose fates were not as wonderful as that of Harley and Star, Bear and I realized that we couldn't save them all. The lesson was a hard one. However, it taught us to give all our horses the chance to lead a long and productive life. We've put many hours into working with horses others have given up on, because we are dedicated to giving these horses a better life. What we feel is even more important is prevention—starting horses off right so that they have every chance to live a healthy life with people who love them.

Take every chance you are given in life, and appreciate and use them to your advantage. More importantly, if someone in your life makes a mistake and he or she is genuinely regretful, give that person a second chance. Second chances allow us to see what someone is capable of, if allowed to grow as a person by trying again. We all deserve a second chance to live a better, more fulfilling life. Always be willing to open your heart to someone who has made a mistake. Forgive that person, because forgiveness is a gift that you give to yourself.

Chapter Eight
Mac and Flower

Finding Your Niche

Through trial and error and second chances, we are able to find our place in life—our niche, so to speak. Jerry Brier, a friendly, outgoing person, showed up at our barn one day, completely unannounced. She asked us to help her find two horses that she would then board at our barn. She and her 12-year-old daughter, Christine, wanted to learn to ride and had gotten our name from someone at the showgrounds located near our barn. Bear and I had lived there for about four or five years, and our daughter Jennifer and I were showing quite a bit at the showgrounds on the weekends. Jerry and her daughter didn't want to compete with their horses; they preferred riding the park trails.

Bear had just finished building us yet another barn, so we had two stalls available. Jerry gave us a budget, and Bear and I went in search of some nice trail horses. We found Mac and Flower almost immediately, and we brought them home. Jerry and her husband, David, were quite pleased with the two horses.

With Mac, looks could be deceiving. He was a big dark horse with a very masculine build, but inside he was a marshmallow—

very sweet and sensitive. Flower was extremely athletic but a little nervous about meeting new people. Let's say, for the sake of argument, that if she were a person, she would be a marching band leader—the one full of energy in the front of the pack that everyone else follows. That was Flower. Don't get me wrong, she was a wonderful horse, but she didn't like to stay in the same place for very long. She was happiest when she was leading a group of horses on a trail, and they all followed at the pace she chose. If you tried to stop her, she would march in place. She respected your space and never forgot her manners, but she couldn't stand still.

Jerry chose to give Flower to her daughter and keep Mac for herself. They would come out every day to brush and groom their horses. With each visit, they brought an endless assortment of treats and gifts. One of the gifts was a baseball cap that said "Mac" across the front. Imagine my surprise when I went to the barn to find big Mac being reduced to wearing a baseball cap with sewn-in ear holes! I dare you to try and convince the most masculine man in your life to wear a pretty pink baseball cap with flowers and his name embroidered on the front.

One day, I was in the house doing some writing when Jerry came running through the back door, saying I *had* to come see what she taught Mac. She announced that she was going to be a trainer and that she was reading all kinds of books about teaching tricks to horses. I set aside what I was doing and followed her outside. She walked into the round pen where Mac was standing, being his gruff, hard-exterior self. He was wearing his wonderful new baseball cap, and all the while, his eyes were pleading, *please get me out of here!* Jerry threw a Frisbee at Mac; it hit him in the face and fell to the ground in front of him. She picked it up and threw it again, swearing that earlier he had caught it in his mouth.

The question that came to mind was not whether he had actually done it, but *why* train a horse to catch a Frisbee? There just seemed to be no logical reason why a person would take the time to teach a horse a trick that had always been reserved for dogs. Why not just buy a dog? After several unsuccessful attempts, she finally gave up.

I smiled and went back into the house. I had met many horses, but I had never met a horse person like Jerry. I didn't see any use in training a horse to catch a Frisbee, but what I realized was that everyone enjoys different activities with their horse. I found Jerry's enthusiasm refreshing, but I must admit that I truly felt for poor Mac.

Although Jerry and her daughter kept their horses' coats shiny, their tails perfectly combed, and their bellies full, they were letting the horses get away with murder. They were wonderful people whose only intentions were to please their equine friends. Unfortunately, Mac began to pick up bad habits, such as trying to break free from the hitching post. Every time he would try, Jerry would unhook him because she couldn't stand to see him struggle, thus rewarding him for unacceptable behavior. Then she bought him a leather breakaway halter that was designed to come apart when he pulled hard enough. This not only made it much easier for him to break free, but, again, it rewarded him for his effort.

In the meantime, Jerry's daughter, Christine, was showing less and less interest in Flower. In fact, she didn't want anything to do with her or any other horse. I had been giving Christine riding lessons and was finding it extremely difficult, because Jerry kept participating in her daughter's lesson. If I asked Christine a question, Jerry would answer it. Jerry audiotaped the lessons and would constantly rewind the tape and ask me to start over because she missed a part. Christine was getting absolutely nothing out of the lesson, and it was becoming increasingly obvious that she didn't want to be there. I finally had a talk with Jerry, and she agreed that I might get further with her daughter if Jerry left during the lesson.

At the next lesson, Jerry dropped Christine off at the barn and left. Christine was very quiet as we saddled up her horse. We worked on basic handling and at first she hesitated to speak at all. Then, much to my surprise, when she did speak, she told me that she was only there because her mother was forcing her to take lessons. She said that I was going to get paid whether she rode her horse or not, so why not let her go into the house and watch television? She would have her mother pay me, and we could keep this to ourselves.

Shocked, I looked at Flower. She was such a nice horse, and Christine was so incredibly lucky to have the opportunity to know her. Yet here she was trying to find a way to get out of riding her. I told Christine that as long as her mother was paying me, she would have two choices: One was to learn safety and riding skills with Flower; the other was to be honest with her mother and tell her that she had no interest in the horse at all. She chose the first option.

Her mother eventually talked Christine into showing at some local shows and even placed her in our 4-H club for a while. I remember the first time she showed Flower at an open show. The class was showmanship, which is judged on one's ability to show the horse by leading it into the class and presenting it to the judge for inspection. It was obvious that Christine didn't want to be there and that Flower had no idea why she was there, either. Christine unhappily stood in the class, and Flower marched around her the entire time. Keep in mind that Flower was the band leader, the enthusiastic, energetic personality with the need to be moving at all times. Christine became frustrated and began to cry.

Jerry was like many other moms, and wanted her daughter to share her interests. But if there is no willingness to do something by either horse or rider, the result is unhappiness. The same holds true for anything that we do in our lives. Neither Christine nor Flower wanted to show.

Horses and riders can learn to enjoy different things in time, but someone has to be the positive-minded leader. If you buy a horse that is suited and trained for trail riding and you are both happy doing it, go trail riding! Should your interests change, find a more suitable horse. If you and your horse are suited for more than one riding principle, by all means, be versatile. Do what feels right, and don't be swayed by pressure from others; you will be much happier as a result.

Even though Jerry seemed enthusiastic about horses, for some reason she never rode Mac. However, Jerry would occasionally convince David, her husband, to ride him instead. He was a nice guy, but a little apprehensive when it came to women teaching him how to do anything. He simply wanted to get on the horse and be left alone. For that reason, I kept to myself except when it came to his possibly getting hurt at our barn.

Since David's visits were few and far between, Jerry asked Bear and me to work with Mac. We took him on long trail rides and taught him the basics. One of the things he was great at was to stop the second we said "Whoa." He was a good horse and learned quickly.

A few weeks after we started working with Mac, David came out to the barn to ride with some of the guys. He and the other men were going to take their horses out on the trails as they had done many times before. David didn't know what progress Mac had made, so I attempted to fill him in. I was particularly concerned over David's ability to ride Mac because David had just had a vasectomy a few days before and probably shouldn't have been riding at all. I also tried to tell him about the new things that Mac had learned, and he ignored me and went off into the woods with the other men, who were all experienced riders.

I watched as the group rode off. David was in a position that we refer to as the *launch position*—toes pointed down in the stirrups, and the body leaning forward. The riders worked their way through the trails in our woods and came out through the open field next to the trees. I heard them galloping next to the woods in the cornfield. I then heard several of the men yell "Whoa!" Just as they did, Mac stopped dead in his tracks, performing probably one of the best sliding stops I had ever seen. When he came to a screeching halt, he launched David forward and up above the saddle. When David came down, he landed not in the seat of the saddle, but rather on the horn.

I could only imagine the level of pain that comes with such a maneuver, especially after having a vasectomy just a few days earlier. I heard several of the men he was riding with groan in pain for having witnessed the landing. Everyone went quiet and watched as David dismounted and walked over and handed the reins to Jerry, who was standing next to me.

"Here," he said, his voice a few octaves higher. Somehow the words "I told you so" were far too cruel, so I quietly excused myself and went into the house, where I laughed hysterically.

We didn't see David at the barn until weeks later. I felt a little bad because he had had a negative experience on a horse. From that point on, David listened more carefully when I had some advice to give him on Mac. The family eventually built their own barn and moved their horses home. I see Christine at shows sometimes with Flower, and the mare still marches in the show ring. Christine has become a good rider, and I truly hope that she has found the joy of horses. I have yet to see Jerry ride Mac. She has now gotten into miniature horses; she dresses them up and takes them to costume classes.

Their family taught me how important it is that we find our own niche. There are so many things you can do with a horse, whether it is jumping, racing, trail riding, or driving. It would be a shame if Jerry had not found the joy of miniature horses. It would seem that this nice family has found its own niche in the world of horses, and they have learned a few lessons of their own. We wish them only the best.

Life is about discovering what makes you happy. Only through discovery can you find your own niche in life. Always be willing to try new things, and don't be afraid to move on to something else that better suits you. Understand that the people in your life may not share your enthusiasm for any particular sport or hobby, and it may tend to become a burden for them (think flowery, pink baseball cap). Appreciate and support the interests of those around you, and accept that everyone's happiness hinges on finding their own niche in life.

Chapter Nine,
This Beau's Eligible

Reaping What You Sow

One October morning, just before Halloween, my husband, Bear, called from work to ask me whether I could go look at a Palomino Quarter Horse that was being sold locally. I rode out to see the horse with veterinarian and friend, Dr. Roger Speiss.

The large, old barn where the horse was kept was only a few repairs short of being quite charming. We drove up to the barn and entered in search of someone. We found a light cream-colored horse, quiet and thin, standing in a stall. As we got closer, we noticed that the horse was holding up a swollen and infected hind leg. The stall was a mess and appeared as though no one had cleaned it in quite some time. There were dried manure stains all over the horse; beneath the filth, you could literally count every rib. I could tell from Roger's sudden change in mood that he was not pleased at seeing a horse treated in this manner. He is not only a good vet but also a racehorse owner, team penner, and roper. He is an experienced horse owner whom I respect very much. We agreed that one of us needed to get the horse out of those conditions.

The condition of the horse made me angry, but I reminded myself to be pleasant when I knocked on the door of the house. I knew that anger wouldn't help the horse in any way. At first, no one answered, and then a woman carrying a baby appeared with two other small children at her side. I told her that I was there to have a look at the horse and she said that she would be right out. I rejoined Roger, and he asked me whether I had known that the horse was a stallion. The ad said only that a Palomino Quarter Horse was for sale and made no reference to the horse's sex category.

Although Bear and I planned on breeding some of our mares someday, having a stallion at our farm was not something that we had ever discussed. There is a specific temperament that is required in handling a stallion properly; a stallion's mentality is so completely different from that of a gelding (a castrated male horse). A stallion is used for breeding, and although one can easily be ridden and shown, it can be difficult to keep a stallion's attention when his focus is on breeding. I had certainly handled other people's stallions, but I didn't know whether I wanted to handle one on a full-time basis. Besides, my daughter Jen and I were showing quite a bit, and each of us already owned our own favorite horses. I had Teddy, my gelding; Bear was working a mare by the name of Thepleasuresallmine (Charlie, for short); and Jen had Philly, a large Appaloosa mare.

The woman came out to answer questions but made it clear that she wouldn't go near the horse. She explained that she was a new horse owner and that other than a pony in the barn, she didn't have any experience with horses. The woman affectionately showed us the pony and filled us in on the stallion's story.

She told us that her husband had gone to an auction and bought the horse for her, not really understanding the differences between owning a stallion and a gelding. He'd thought the horse, named This Beau's Eligible (Beau for short), was pretty, so he bought him. The woman told us that she had once tried to ride him through an open field and all he did was buck. She said she couldn't handle him because he would "go crazy." Beau did seem a little anxious, but by no means crazy. Because she was so afraid of him, the woman now left him in his stall all day and let her husband deal with him when he got home. By the fact that he was extremely underweight, it was obvious that no one, not even the husband, was tending to his nutritional needs. This was the reason he was for sale. The owner honestly seemed like a nice person, just one who was ignorant of what it takes to own a stallion.

Roger asked her how he had hurt his leg and she proceeded to tell us that he was out of control, so she tied him up with a logging chain to her pickup truck. I could see the chain laying on the ground in the driveway. I shuddered at the thought of the poor horse bearing the weight of the heavy metal chain.

We stood outside of Beau's stall and discussed his personality. He was leaning against the stall wall and every once in a while, would half rear up in an attempt to see the pony in the next stall. I knew Beau was acting like any stallion would with a mare next door. I hated to leave because I knew that, out of fear, the owner may not clean his stall or tend to his wounds. She didn't have any corrals in which to put him, so we moved the pony to another stall and put Beau in a nice, clean, ten-by-ten stall until I could come back.

I thought the price she wanted for him was high, but it was what her husband had paid for him at the auction. She knew that he was not in the best of shape now, but thought that she should be able to find someone to buy him for what they had paid. I asked her if she would be more comfortable with an easygoing gelding. She assured me that all she needed was a horse that she could go for a ride on and not have to fight with as much. She wanted a slow trail ride on a horse who would listen. She said she would be willing to trade Beau for a horse if she got along with it.

What I had in mind was a gelding named Joker whom we had been riding for a few months. He was quiet and gentle and seemed perfect for what she needed. He had come to our place a little skittish because he had been handled roughly. However, with a little time, he transformed into a willing and calm horse.

I needed to speak with Bear about possibly trading Joker for the stallion, so I kept my thoughts to myself and told the woman that I would call her in the afternoon. When Roger dropped me off later that day, I called Bear, and he agreed that we should suggest a trade or find another way to get Beau.

I believed that Beau's owner was a genuinely good person who just wanted to enjoy a horse. I hoped that if she had one that she was more comfortable with, she would take proper care of it. We made arrangements for this woman and her husband to come over and ride Joker a couple of times to see whether he was a horse she could handle. To our delight, they seemed to click, and we made the trade. We talked to them extensively about Joker's care and handling. It eased my mind to see her dedication and fondness for her new horse. I was dedicated to ensuring the happiness of Joker after she took him home, and I offered to help out in any way I could. One of the conditions of the trade was that she must immediately put up a corral so she could turn Joker out to get some exercise. The last thing we wanted was for Joker to end up in the same condition as Beau.

We continued to call his new owner once a week to make sure she was doing all right with Joker. She assured us that he was doing well and that she was thrilled to be riding him—almost every day. It would seem that she had found her niche; a horse that suited her personality. We continued to check on how things were going with them because we had a responsibility to make sure Joker was with a family who would care for him. She had indeed put up a corral and lived up to that part of the promise.

We brought Beau home and started to get him in better shape: We treated the infection in his leg, and put him on a regular feeding schedule. His condition began to improve immediately. We spent that winter concentrating on Beau. Bear and I decided to work on getting him back in shape before we started him under saddle. He didn't seem like a stallion at all. Nevertheless, we agreed that Jen wouldn't handle him under any circumstances and that if he proved too much for Bear and me to handle, we would have him gelded.

Although we could literally count every rib from quite a distance, eventually we watched as Beau transformed into the most awesome-looking horse that we had ever seen. His coat was a dark golden color, and with the exercise and constant work on ground manners, he was building up tons of muscle.

When we'd brought him home, Beau's former owner had given me a manila envelope with paperwork in it. Until this point, we had concentrated more on the horse than the registration papers. Finally, I went through the envelope and realized that this horse was out of a horse that Bear and I had always admired—Great Pine. Great Pine was his Grand sire on one side and the Grand sire on the other side was American Quarter Horse Association (AQHA) halter horse, Beau Bonanza. Great Pine was a legend.

I called Larry Rose, Great Pine's owner, and he couldn't have been nicer about answering my questions. He even gave me the phone number of the man who last owned Beau. I called and asked the previous owner why he had sold Beau, and he explained that he was forced to sell him because of his divorce. It was nice to know that Beau wasn't sold because of any unsoundness or behavioral problem.

Larry gave me one of the best pieces of advice that Bear and I had received on handling a stallion. He said that, no matter how well behaved he is, it is important that we never drop our guard with him because stallions are very unpredictable creatures. Unlike geldings and mares, the ever-present instinct to breed often shortens their attention span.

I thanked Larry for his insight and spent the next several weeks researching the other horses in Beau's pedigree. Bear got more help from the owner of Beau's sire, Ima Ripe Bonanza. She had accomplished quite a bit with her horse and although she didn't know Beau personally, she assured us that he had come from excellent stock. Names such as Wimpy, Leo, King, Poco Bueno, and other Quarter Horse legends kept coming up in his pedigree. He was already registered with the AQHA as well as the Palomino Horse Breeders Association (PHBA). We contacted the National Foundation Quarter Horse Association (NFQHA) and inquired as to his percentage of foundation bloodlines. The foundation bloodlines and percentages thereof determine how many of the original respected Quarter Horses he was related to before breeders began cross breeding to Thoroughbred horses for speed and size. They told us that he could be registered as 94 percent, a phenomenal rating. The NFQHA was a fairly new registry at the time, and it listed Beau in the very first studbook of the association.

In the meantime, we were still calling Joker's owner on a weekly basis. We were assured each time that things were fine and that they were riding him every day. She didn't need our assistance, so our curiosity made us drive by now and then to see that he was turned out. We saw him out occasionally on sunny days, and he looked good.

Spring arrived and with it came what I refer to as the "fight of our lives." It seemed that the stronger Beau became physically, the more his overall attitude changed and the harder it was to contend with his ever-increasing energy. We found it difficult to keep his attention focused on us and what we were trying to achieve.

Beau's constant challenges were killing us, and the strides that we were making in calming this horse down seemed few and far between. The more we tried to get him back in shape, the more strength he had to use against us.

After months of constant, difficult work, one day everything we had been trying to teach him seemed to finally click. I was watching Bear work Beau in the round pen; it was as if Beau suddenly realized that we were there. He didn't look through us, but rather at us. He immediately began to respond. I felt as if something specific had caused the transformation, but I could only credit Bear's patience and persistence.

Once we had made the breakthrough, Beau learned very quickly. He would walk next to us and when we stopped, he would stop; when we backed up, he backed up. When we turned toward him, he would pivot on his hind leg. It took my breath away; he would lean back on those powerful hindquarters and spin just as fast as I could walk. He reminded me so much of Hollywood, a beautiful palomino who had belonged to my old friend Jack Osgerby.

Beau seemed to like me and never tried to bite or hurt me in any way. He was a pleasure until I would lose his attention. Once I lost his attention, it was as though I didn't exist. I spent hours some days in the barn with him trying to earn his trust. I would brush him and walk him and give him all of my attention just to establish his respect of my space.

We rode him every chance we got, sometimes turning on the lights in the round pen so we could work him in the late evening. At first, we wanted to keep him slow in his gaits so that we could perfect each one. Speed is nothing without control. Control must come first. Everything that we learn in working with horses is collected and referred to as *tools*. We used absolutely every training tool that we had learned and collected over the years in order to face the challenges Beau presented.

Mutual respect and cooperation were the two most important things. They would be the foundation for everything we would eventually do with Beau. I believe that the results that you receive are based on the time that you spend. Developing anything in your life is rather like planting a seed and watching it grow. You have to be willing to care for what you plant by nurturing it, and we were certainly doing this with Beau. As the saying goes, "You reap what you sow," and we knew that if we worked hard enough with this horse, our efforts would reward us in so many ways.

One day, Bear was out working with Beau. It had snowed the night before and now the sun was melting the fluffy white snow into a slippery, slushy mess. Bear found one of the quick-fix gadgets somewhere in the barn and decided to use it. (Pieces of equipment of this nature are often used as shortcuts to achieving control, but I personally am not a big fan of quick fixes.) It was a *running martingale,* and its purpose is to pull the horse's head in a lower position by directing all pressure from the reins toward the rings in the martingale. The biggest problem with a running martingale is that *all* pressure from the reins is directed downward. I warned Bear that it would be best if he used the martingale only for short periods of time and only in a controlled area. Bear started in the round pen and was having such wonderful results that he decided to ride Beau out into the yard. Jen and I were sitting in the kitchen when we saw Bear and Beau come around the corner of the house.

The two mares in the front corral immediately distracted Beau's attention. He called out to them. They responded by coming closer to the fence, pacing and calling back. Beau started to dance around, putting on a show for the mares. The mares were in season (for breeding) and Beau had tunnel vision. To Beau, Bear no longer existed and the reins were merely an inconvenience. His only objective was to reach the mares. Beau's next maneuver was to buck, harder than I had ever seen any horse buck before. Bear tried desperately to get Beau's head up so that he couldn't buck, but he couldn't because the martingale directed all pressure from the reins downward and backward. The martingale served as an aid for Beau to drop his head further, thus allowing him to buck harder.

I was sure both horse and rider were going to flip as we watched Beau's nose actually touch the snow. There was a rodeo right outside my kitchen window! Beau would buck, and Bear would try in vain to pull his head up. Then Beau would spin, and Bear would try desperately to hold on so he didn't get thrown in the snow. Bear took the first opportunity to get off and got him back under control. I have never seen a man dismount a horse that quickly. After he had Beau calmed down and listening again, he ended on a good note and put Beau away.

Bear came through the front door, threw the martingale on the floor, and yelled, "Burn this piece of junk, and call Roger and have that horse gelded!" All I could do was laugh. I knew that after he had cooled down and gave it some thought, he would realize that it wasn't the martingale or even the horse that was at fault in this situation: It was his own desire to take shortcuts and ask the horse to do something that he just couldn't handle yet.

Until Beau came to live with us, his purpose in life had been to stand out in the pasture and look pretty. Then he was sent to people who had no concept of his needs and responded to his behavior by tying him to the bumper of a truck with a chain. Now, with hard work and patience, he was well on his way to becoming a well-behaved stallion—but he wasn't there quite yet.

We had our hands full, that was for sure, but after working with Beau for six months we knew he was capable of being a good, sound, trustworthy horse. Once again, we had had to ask ourselves whether we were up to the task. Every day was a challenge, and every single thing we did with this horse brought a new situation that put our skills to the test. I never called Roger, nor did I burn the martingale. Bear finally calmed down and started working with Beau again. This time he took no shortcuts.

Eventually, Beau behaved well enough that it was a pleasure to work with him. He would still regress now and then, but for the most part, we continued to move forward. We were excited with his progress, so we decided to take him to a Palomino show in Hilliard, Ohio. Even though Bear and I were extremely nervous, Beau could not have behaved better. It was a double-judged, A-circuit show, which is a pretty big deal, but we were sure that he was ready. The judges loved him. We came home that day with Reserve Champion Stallion, having placed either first or second in all the color and halter classes.

Beau hadn't been under saddle long enough to ride him in any classes, so we continued to show him in halter for the experience with horses and crowds, and for the points. He did wonderfully, and we actually earned enough points to qualify for the Palomino Horse Breeders Association World Show in Tulsa, Oklahoma. We continued riding Beau at home that summer, and he became so docile that Jen could ride him under our close supervision. Our hard work had paid off, and it was time to reap the rewards.

With the success in the show ring, people began asking about breeding Beau to their mares. We wanted to breed him to mares eventually, but we didn't want to risk losing the strides that we had made with his training. We decided to try breeding to just a few mares and see how he responded. We bred exactly three mares late that spring: our own mare, Thepleasuresallmine (Charlie), and two others. Other than the three breedings, we concentrated on getting ready for the upcoming show season.

The World Show came quickly, and we packed up and headed for Tulsa. We drove for seventeen hours in a borrowed motor home, towing a two-horse trailer. Beau was tired, but he handled the long trip better than we had ever expected. We would look out the back window, and he would be playing with his lead rope or watching the trucks go by on the highway. We had a tire blowout just outside of Tulsa, and he stood there calmly while we changed the tire. Beau was well prepared and relaxed.

I was the one who qualified Beau, so I would be the one to show him. I was extremely nervous because it was my first World Show, and I had no idea what to expect. I couldn't sleep all the way there because I was so excited. We arrived at 3 a.m. The showgrounds were huge, and I suddenly felt anxious. I worried so much that we weren't ready and that we may be a bit out of our league. I was living my dream, but I wondered on some level why we had come halfway across the country to show a horse that had once been kept tied to the bumper of someone's pickup truck with a logging chain. We had extremely high hopes for him, regardless of his humble beginnings.

As we walked to our assigned stall, there were yellow horses for as far as the eye could see. After we got Beau settled in for the night, we were too excited to go to bed, so we went and got Jen and her friend Elizabeth a golf cart and turned them loose to check out the grounds. Bear and I went to see the arena that I would be showing in later that day. It was a large indoor arena, and I walked the route I would be taking. I went from the practice arena through a hallway and into the biggest indoor arena I had ever seen. There would be four judges, and the pattern would be to walk to the first judge, trot past him, turn and then walk to the next judge, and so on until I had passed all four judges. Then I would line up head to tail across the arena and set up Beau for inspection by the four judges. It always helps me if I walk my pattern before the class so that I know the steps and there are no surprises. I had it all figured out in my head.

We went to collect Jen and Elizabeth, who had somehow wedged the golf cart between the barn wall and the corner of a stall. They were laughing hysterically because they'd had no sleep, and although neither of them knew how to drive, they were trying to maneuver a golf cart. We made them go get some rest since our class wouldn't be until later that morning. Bear slept for a while as well, but I couldn't.

I wanted to take it all in. This was a dream I had wanted to achieve since I was very young. I visited with Beau, who was now sound asleep in a corner of his stall, and brushed his tail and whispered to him. None of the excitement had bothered Beau at all. His confident and calm presence reminded me of why I was here.

As the sun came up, people multiplied until there was a steady roar of excitement. It was a hot, muggy July day that just kept getting hotter. I have never experienced greater misery than 98-degree weather, with 100 percent humidity, in Tulsa, Oklahoma, wearing show clothes. My jacket was heavily lined and my makeup was melting as soon as I applied it. Bear and Jen were putting the final touches on Beau as we walked into the practice area. He was calm; I was still a little nervous, but ready. Bear and Jen left me in line to go back into the huge grandstands to watch.

Certain types of horses are popular at certain times, and the popular type of horse at the time was taller, with more of a Thoroughbred influence. However, the stocky, albeit small, foundation-bred Quarter Horse, such as Beau, was growing in popularity. The judges could go either way in their decision. I believe that if you qualify for a show like the World Show, you take the opportunity and go. The learning experience and the adventure of the trip will far outweigh any ribbon or lack thereof. Whatever the outcome, Beau had earned his place in the row of stallions that day.

To enter the arena, Beau and I had to walk into a small hallway that led from outside. There was a stallion in front of me and one behind me. Just as we entered the hallway, a blast of air-conditioning offered welcome relief from the heat.

We presented to each of the judges and went to line up, head to tail, with the other horses in the class. As they announced the placing, I had no grand expectations, but we placed third under one judge and fourth under the other three! We were ecstatic! I could hear Bear and Jen hollering from the audience as we stepped up to receive our ribbons.

I felt bad leading Beau back outside into the heat, but after our pictures were taken, we washed him down and put him back in the cool of the barn with some water and hay.

We headed home the next morning. By the time we got home, we were all exhausted. Fulfilling your dreams is a good kind of tired. We had worked hard and placed at the World Show. All the time, challenges, and constant battles had been worth it. Beau was our opportunity to take a horse, work with him, and see how far he could go. Beau was a diamond in the rough, and to have the opportunity to let him shine was such a blessing for all of us.

We had a stallion that was in the top five Palomino stallions in the world! The realization of our accomplishments became more apparent after we left the ring. Two of the judges came up to us later that day and complimented us on Beau's beauty and grace. One of them went so far as to say that he would have placed him first if he had just had a little more muscle on him. Beau's show ring success helped us decide that it was time to plan our breeding program with him.

For all that he has given us, Beau deserves a comfortable lifestyle, and we have always seen to it that he is treated with the utmost respect. He taught us what it takes to achieve dreams: persistence and patience. These two very valuable tools will serve you well in every aspect of your life. You reap what you sow—and the harvest is certainly worth the effort.

Chapter Ten
Joker

Regret

*I*t doesn't matter who you are or what you do in your life, at some point, you are going to do something you will most likely regret for the rest of your life. A life without regret is a life not lived to the fullest. I believe everyone has some level of regret in life because if you have no regret, you have no conscience.

Trust is something that should not be given lightly, and yet when it is given, you balance on a fine line between setting yourself up for disappointment and having faith in another human being. Horses are trusting animals by nature. They go into every relationship with an open mind and a clean slate. Once that trust is taken too lightly, however, it is difficult to regain it. This is a story not only of trust and disappointment between people but also, unfortunately, of the misuse of trust between horse and human.

There are basically two ways to train a horse, in my opinion. One is to figure out what makes the horse tick, use patience and kindness, and make the horse your partner. This method is like a dance, and to make the dance spectacular, you and your partner have to anticipate each other's moves and respond accordingly. There has to be trust and the ability to move in unison both physically and mentally. Working with a horse is no different than building a relationship. If you want a good relationship with someone, consider it a dance; you will realize that every step you take is one more step toward making it spectacular.

The other method to train a horse is by using force and fear to break the horse's spirit. Bear and I have watched many people use this technique, and we agree that there is always one thing in common in the personalities of the handlers, one factor that drives them to bring a horse to total submission: fear. You can see it in the eyes of both the horse and the handler. Fear in the handler breeds fear in the horse. Many years ago, when I watched my father and two other men lay down a horse and force him into total submission, I was so frightened I literally could not breathe because I could feel the horse's fear. But there was no fear in those men's eyes that day; there was absolutely no aggressive force involved. It was a horse whom someone at some time had taken almost to the point of no return. That horse trusted no one. In order to bring the horse back to a point where the men could work with him, they had to start over. Once the horse was laid down, they offered him comfort. It was the beginning of a beautiful relationship with the horse.

We saw fear in Joker's eyes the day we met him. We had room for another horse at the barn, so we went to meet Joker at a nearby facility. He was turned out in an indoor arena when we arrived. The handler raised his hand to try to grab the horse and Joker's eyes went wild, his head immediately reared up, and he backed away from his handler. The handler called the horse "crazy" and chased him off with a whip until he stopped in the dark corner of the indoor arena, where the entire process began again.

Bear asked whether he could be left alone to check the horse out. The handler agreed and excused himself. There was a certain calmness that immediately came over Joker as soon as the handler was out of sight. Jen, our youngest daughter, and I watched as Bear quietly stood in the center of the arena and waited for the horse to come to him. It took a while but eventually Joker realized that Bear wasn't there to hurt him and got curious enough to approach. Finally, Joker nudged Bear's arm, and Joker dropped his head. Bear took this cue to touch the horse. Joker tensed but didn't back away. Bear spoke to him in a gentle voice as he stroked his shoulder. Unfortunately, just as everything was going well, the handler returned, and Joker immediately retreated to his safe dark corner of the arena.

There was hope; we could see it in the horse's eyes. Bear and I agreed to take the horse home and spend some time with him. We wanted to see whether we could somehow erase the damage that had been done. We caught and loaded the horse, paid the owner his asking price, and took our new horse home.

Joker acted like quite a few horses we had met, but worse. It took much longer to settle him than it had other horses because he was afraid. He didn't trust us one bit, despite our kindness toward him. We patiently waited for him to come around. He lived in the round pen for the first several weeks so that he could move around yet have the opportunity to come to us if he chose. We didn't want to force him to trust us, so our only option was to give him every opportunity we could to understand that he had no reason to fear us. We ignored him when he kept his distance and praised him when he ventured close.

Joker needed to find his confidence with people, so we gave him the illusion that he was running the show—no force, just attention when *he* chose to give it. It didn't take long before he was meeting us at the gate as we arrived instead of hiding in the corner. The more he regained his confidence, the more he showed us what he was capable of doing, and the more we started seeing how much fun he was. As with people, there are no shortcuts to building trust. We took our time and ended up with a trusting animal who would give you everything he had when it came time to work.

Eventually, Bear and I agreed that Joker was ready to move on as soon as we found the right person. As if by fate, we met Beau, our stallion. When the woman who was interested in trading Beau for Joker came over to ride, Joker responded to her better than he did with any of us. We had her come back a second time and spoke to her at great length about his needs and how important it would be for her and her family to continue to be patient with him and earn his trust. She reassured us that he was exactly what she wanted, and we made the trade.

We called Joker's new owners often and, each time, the woman would tell us how well Joker was doing and how they were riding him every day. She said that things were just perfect. We drove by often, but did not stop, for fear that we would be invading their privacy. We could see Joker out in the corral from the road, and he looked good. We traded Joker in October and kept in touch with the woman well into the beginning of the following year. Each time, she would assure us that everything was fine and that she was riding him almost every day. She said she loved him and was spoiling him rotten.

One rainy, chilly day in late April, we got a call from an extremely upset friend. She knew Joker well and was very fond of him. She said that Joker was at some man's barn and that the man had decided that the horse was "crazy," had beaten him, and was now trying to get him loaded in the trailer to take him to auction. We told our friend that this couldn't possibly be the same horse because he was over at this woman's barn and everything was going well. We told our friend how each time we spoke to Joker's owner, she told us how well he was doing. But she insisted that it was Joker and gave us directions to the man's barn. She begged us to hurry if we were going to save the horse.

We were at a total loss for words. Bear and I stood in our kitchen with another friend of ours. We made a group decision to call Joker's owner and ask her outright whether she had sold the horse. Her husband answered the phone. Bear asked how things were going and he told us that everything was fine and how very much they loved the horse. Now we were more confused.

We decided that Bear and his friend would go over to the barn where Joker was supposedly being beaten and see what horse they were referring to. On the way, they would swing by Joker's barn and see whether they could see him. Since it was raining, the horses would most likely be in the barn, but he would check anyway, and then head to the barn where the Joker look-alike was being forced into the trailer. He took with him every bit of cash we had, in case Joker actually needed rescuing.

Approximately an hour later, the guys came down the driveway with Joker banging around in the trailer behind them. When Bear had arrived at the barn, the man was literally beating Joker in an attempt to load him in the trailer. Bear made a deal with the man, who was in a predicament, since he could not handle the horse well enough to load him and haul him away. Bear gave the man all the cash we had and bought Joker. Bear had led Joker to our trailer, and he walked right in. Joker banged in the trailer all the way home and when Bear unloaded him, he was thin and scared. The look in his eyes led us to believe that there was every possibility that we would never be able to reach him again.

It was sad to see him that way after seeing what a sweet horse he had become. We had trusted Joker's owner to care for him, when all the while she had been lying to us. We'd made every effort to see to it that Joker was well cared for, and here he was back with us and we were back to square one. After we got him settled in the barn, Bear picked up the phone and called the woman once more. This time, she answered the phone. Bear clenched his jaw as he asked her how Joker was doing. She proceeded to lie to him in great detail about how everything was fine and she was riding him every day, and he was happy and healthy. We were just awestruck.

If she had called us, we would have helped in any way we could. Bear told her that we knew that she had sold the horse two months earlier and that she had been lying to us all that time.

We kept Joker for some time after that and made him our pet project. He trusted us and he had trusted this woman, and we knew we would have to work hard to earn that trust again. He did finally come around, and the next time we placed him, we made sure that it was with good people in a great home. After all these years, we are still able to check in on him from time to time because he has the same owners who bought him from us. He has a good life.

There will inevitably be a situation where you will regret a decision that you've made. We were lucky enough to fix the mistake we made with Joker, although I can't take away the pain Joker felt when he was in the wrong hands.

Joker taught us that using force and fear are the quickest ways to ruin a trusting horse, but that a horse's spirit can be rekindled with patience and kindness. As with horses, you will meet people who have lost their ability to trust, for whatever reason, but it, too, can be rekindled with patience and love. Trust is earned by both animals and people and should never be taken lightly. Regret is an unavoidable fact of life. The best thing to do is try to fix the situation as well as you can, learn from your mistakes, and move on.

Chapter Eleven
Charlie

Facing Adversity

*F*aith is a funny thing. Faith in yourself, faith in God, or faith in anything that you trust can be shaken when faced with adversity. I find it ironic that it's usually when we need faith the most that we lose it. It is at the darkest times in our lives that we need to hold on to our faith as tightly as we can. If we can manage to do this, it will see us through. Life isn't fair; the simple truth is that bad things happen in life, and there seems to be no rhyme or reason. Adversity is merely a test of your strength, your faith, and your ability to survive it.

Thepleasuresallmine—or Charlie, as we called her—is the horse that tested our faith. It wouldn't be the last time—far from it—but this horse taught me that bad things happen, and she gave me strength for what would lie ahead in our lives. Indeed, there couldn't have been a more fitting name for this mare. I can honestly say that aside from our two daughters and me, Charlie is most likely the love of Bear's (my husband's) life.

In the late 1990s, through a friend of a friend, Bear received a call one morning from a woman in Michigan who desperately needed help with her five horses. Kay was the nicest woman we had ever met. She loved her horses and gave them the best of everything. However, despite her good intentions, she had spoiled her little herd rotten. She had never really insisted on ground manners when they were young, and, as a result, they admittedly walked all over her. She wanted Bear and me to come out to her barn and help her decide which horses she should keep. She wanted to keep one for herself and one for her young daughter, and then find homes for the other three.

When we entered the barn, Kay was feeding the horses and getting ready to put them away for the night, so we offered to help. When we opened the pasture gate to get the first horse, they all pushed past us and ran to the barn as though we deserved no respect at all. They were used to just letting themselves in, and each knew which stall was his. It resembled children coming in from recess as the bell rang. As the horses went barreling past, we got our first look at her herd. They were five very nice-looking horses. The last one in the barn was a pretty little sorrel mare with the sweetest eyes I had ever seen. Even though they had poor manners, all of the horses would be easy for her to sell. They were well cared for, and it showed. Bear and I spent some time working the horses on the ground and got to know them a little. The sorrel mare, although sweet, had even fewer manners than the others.

Kay, Bear, and I went to the house and spent the evening talking about horses. We asked a lot of questions about each horse and realized right away which two were perfect for the woman and her daughter. The little sorrel wasn't one of them. We also spoke about what Kay would need to do to get these horses to the point where she would be able to safely handle and keep them. Kay and Bear hit it off immediately, and she was impressed with his way with the horses. He had easily bonded with her horses, and Kay couldn't ask enough questions.

The next day, Kay called and said that she wanted Bear to come and get the little sorrel. She knew that he really liked the horse and wanted him to have her. There were no strings attached, she simply wanted the little mare to have a good home. Bear was ecstatic. We went to pick up the mare, and Kay signed her over to him.

We gave the mare the barn name of Charlie because she had a pretty, tomboy personality. She was sweet, and in her eyes, you could see that she was a thinker. Although her ground manners needed a lot of work, she loved the attention we gave her and was willing to learn. We led her to and from the barn each day, and she learned that she was not allowed to invade our space by walking all over us. She was expected to walk at her handler's pace and to stand immediately next to us as we led her.

When we started her under saddle, however, she was the most difficult horse we had ever started. She just didn't like the confinement of a saddle. Our method of starting a horse under saddle begins with quietly rubbing her with the saddle pad, bridle, and ropes to be sure she is accustomed to things touching her entire body. We then pony her, or lead her while we are riding another horse, to get her used to having people at a level above her. Then we put the saddle on her, cinching it a little at a time, and walk her a few steps, repeating the process until the saddle is tight enough that it will not fall. Once it is tight enough to stay on if the horse bucks, we place the horse on the longe line and allow her time to get used to the weight of the saddle and cinch before we add our own weight. The entire process usually takes anywhere from ten to twenty minutes, depending on the horse, and we are usually successfully mounting the horse with the saddle fully cinched in under an hour.

This method had worked wonderfully for many horses, with each one bucking just a bit, and then settling in and accepting the saddle with little trouble. Not Charlie. She was all right until we began to cinch the saddle even a little. She immediately blew, taking out a couple of rails in the round pen. She would carry on until she got the saddle off, and we would begin again. The cycle would start all over.

Charlie didn't show any signs of panic, pain, or fear; she simply did not want to wear a saddle. Once the saddle was on the ground, she would walk over to us as if to say, "I'm sorry, I'm just not interested in this." At no time did we use force on her. With patience and persistence, we came to an understanding that, until she allowed us to saddle, cinch, and mount her, we were not finished. After several hours, we had the saddle in place.

Native Americans would ride their horses in the water to teach them to accept a rider, because it is difficult for a horse to buck while standing in water. The pressure of the water made it nearly impossible for them to make much of a fuss at all. Once the horse calmed down, the rider would ride the horse out of the water. I wished I had a pond. But even without one, Charlie accepted a rider fairly quickly.

It is our theory that horses will do what is expected of them if they understand what it is you are asking. If the handler communicates clearly with the horse, the horse will understand and, with few exceptions, will cooperate. Communication is the key to any good relationship; being clear about what you are trying to communicate to anyone is incredibly important.

We waited a while to see whether Charlie would have any physical or mental problems. We attributed her difficulty in training only to her wisdom. She was a thinker. We were lucky to have been given a healthy, happy mare. We decided she would make a good riding mare and a great broodmare. She was beautiful and had all the qualities that we were looking for in a mare to breed to Beau, our Palamino Quarter Horse.

We told Kay that we were considering breeding the mare to Beau, and she said to have her thoroughly checked out by a vet. The first thing we did was to call our vet, Roger, and have him come out and have a look at the mare. Then we called for a second opinion from a vet who specialized in equine reproduction. After careful consideration and thorough tests, that vet proclaimed that Charlie was fine and it was all right to breed her.

This would be the first mare that we ever bred to Beau, and it would be a new experience for us. It took time to learn how to safely prepare and handle both mare and stallion, and our research paid off. We were successful the first time we bred her. Once bred, we were delighted to find that pregnancy suited Charlie. Both her physical appearance and her behavior became more wonderful than it had ever been.

We wanted to do everything possible to know that we were going to have a healthy foal. Roger had confirmed that Charlie was bred through a physical exam, but we wanted to be sure. Roger didn't yet have ultrasound equipment, so we called another vet. Our practice has always been to ultrasound at least once, twice if possible, to see that everything is going well. Depending on whom you ask, some will tell you that ultrasounds are not necessary at all, while others will tell you that several ultrasounds are required. With our opinion at the time, an ultrasound at approximately eighteen to twenty-one days was necessary to ensure that the mare was indeed bred and that everything was going well. If there was any doubt that the pregnancy was anything other than a healthy single fetus, or if there was any question as to the health of the mare, we would perform a second ultrasound at approximately forty-five days.

I was there during the first ultrasound, and everything looked great. The vet told us that Charlie was coming along nicely and from the size of the fetus, she would be giving birth to a healthy foal sometime in April, about ten months away. A mare is usually pregnant for approximately 340 days, but, as with people, can be pregnant for longer or give birth sooner. We asked whether there was any reason to have the vet come down and check the mare again. He assured us that she was doing wonderfully, and, unless there was any change in her behavior, he felt that the second ultrasound wasn't necessary.

We were very excited at the prospect of this foal because it would be both Beau and Charlie's first foal. We continued to monitor Charlie's feed, weight, and overall condition, and as Christmas came and went, we found ourselves anticipating spring and the birth of her foal.

Just after Christmas, we took Jen and her friends to the movies. It was during the holiday break, and we decided to go do something fun. Charlie was turned out with another mare in the front pasture, and, when we left, she was eating some hay and playing with the other horse. We had a wonderful time at the movies and returned just a few hours later to find Charlie pacing the fence line with her tail raised and her body sweating. It was beginning to get dark, but we could see she was obviously upset about something. Upon closer examination, we discovered she had a bloody discharge and immediately knew something was wrong. I called Roger, and he told me that he would be over, but that if it had progressed to that point, chances were she was already losing the foal and there really wasn't much that could be done. He said to put her in the barn and keep her comfortable, and he would stop by as soon as he could.

After putting the horses away, it occurred to us that Charlie could have already lost the foal, so Bear went out to the front pasture with a flashlight and began to look around. I watched out the window as he stopped at the front corner of the fence and bent down. He stayed there for a few minutes, and then walked toward the house. He came in the front door and told me not to go out as he was sure I didn't want to see what was there. Bear called Roger again to tell him that it was too late. I grabbed my boots and coat and headed out the door.

I honestly wish I had listened to Bear, because he was right when he said that I would not be ready for what I found. In the snow were not one but two dead foals, both beautiful and both palomino in color. It is an image that I will never be able to erase from my mind.

Charlie had been carrying undetected twins and had lost them both. Twins are not uncommon in horses; however, carrying them to term is very rare. Bear buried the twins in the front pasture and we were left with the "if only's" and "what if's" that come with loss. Although the grief was unbearable, we had to turn our attention to Charlie and get her through the complications that sometimes come with foaling too early. Roger came out and gave her a strong antibiotic and oxitocin, a drug that causes contractions and is used in expelling any remaining afterbirth.

For the next two weeks, we were faced with every possible complication that could arise. Charlie stopped eating and drinking, showed signs of colic, and ran a fever, which told us that there was an infection present. Roger practically lived at our barn, doing anything humanly possible to save the mare. Bear and I took turns walking her and sitting in the stall with her, giving her strong antibiotics. We were tired, but nothing else in the world mattered except saving the mare.

Charlie had come to mean so much to all of us, but especially to Bear. She was the love of his life. We know so many people who turn their horses out and let nature take its course, and these horses consistently produce healthy babies. Here we were, two of the most discriminate people we knew, seeing to it that our horses have their shots, are wormed regularly, and are monitored closely. Yet, we had lost the foals, and now we risked losing Charlie.

What if we had insisted on a second ultrasound? For that matter, what if we had never bred her at all? These thoughts haunted us through the long hours and the sleepless nights, when the only thing we could do in the darkness of the barn was think. Just when we thought all hope was lost, we received a little ray of hope. It had been two weeks to the day that we had lost the foals, and one morning, Charlie just started eating and drinking. She seemed to be regaining strength. Roger showed up, as he had almost every morning, and examined her. Things were looking brighter. We brushed her, and later that afternoon, we turned her out in the round pen to get a little fresh air and some sunshine. The day was beautiful and although it was cold, the winds had died down and the sun was out. As the day went on, she looked better and better.

Roger called to tell us that he was hauling his horse over to Roberts Arena to ride and to call if we needed him. He had been with us through the whole ordeal, and we told him to go and have fun. We decided to celebrate Charlie's breakthrough with Chinese food. Bear and Jen headed for town, and I stayed behind to take a well-needed hot bath. I went to the barn to check on the mare several times, and she looked good. When Bear and Jen returned, we ate and made phone calls to tell everyone who had supported us that Charlie had taken a turn for the better.

Bear went out to check on Charlie again at about 7:30 that evening, and she was down in her stall and thrashing. He got her up and hollered to the house to get Roger back out here. He took her in the round pen and began walking her. I called the Roberts Arena where Roger was, and I told them to send him out right away. I found out later that Roger had handed his horse off to someone and left without so much as a word. We had come to rely on him, and he never let us down.

After I hung up the phone, I went out in the round pen to find that Charlie had gone into shock. Bear was trying desperately to get her on her feet. He had every blanket we owned covering her to keep her from shaking. The stress from the previous two weeks had taken its toll, not only on Charlie, but also on Bear, and he was falling apart before my eyes. If his will had been enough to keep that mare from dying, she would still be alive today. We tried to get her to stand, but to no avail. At the moment of her death, Bear's sorrow echoed through the bare trees that stood cold and quiet beyond the round pen where she lay. He sobbed, heartbroken, kneeling with his face against his beautiful mare.

At the time, neither of us had ever experienced the pain of such a loss. I felt totally powerless the night Charlie died. Hearing the pain and anger in Bear's voice as he pleaded with her not to go made me realize how powerless we really are to change the bad things that happen in our lives.

We had bred only three mares that first year, Charlie and two others. They were all bred at approximately the same time. The second mare, Cocoa, belonged to Pat and George Shudel, dear friends of ours; and the third mare belonged to a client.

While we were dealing with the grief of our own loss, we received a call from the Shudels. They told us that Cocoa had died of colic that was unrelated to her pregnancy. This was a hard blow to take. We had shifted our hopes from Charlie's foal to Cocoa's, in hope that the birth of her foal would lift our spirits. Now both Cocoa and her foal were gone. A short time later, we were awakened by a phone call from the third mare owner, telling us that their barn had caught fire during the night and they had lost several horses. One of them was their mare, the third one we had bred. Three mares, all bred to the same stallion—and all three died for different but equally devastating reasons. It seemed no matter where we placed our hope, it was shattered. That is the interesting thing about hope—it gets you through the tough times in life, and yet it can also be the source of such disappointment.

That winter was the coldest either Bear or I could remember. Not so much because of the actual temperature, but because each time we refocused our hopes, they were shattered. If we'd ever thought of just walking away from horses, it was that winter. After a lot of soul-searching, we decided that we just didn't have it in us to walk away, so we started over. We focused on Beau and concentrated on the future breeding season. From that point on, we decided that regardless of the outcome of the first ultrasound at eighteen to twenty-one days, we would always have a second one at forty-five days, if for no other reason than our peace of mind. There would always be an emptiness in our hearts for Charlie and her foals, and Bear would always miss her. Our faith got us through a really horrible winter, and at last, spring came and that heartbreaking winter was behind us.

As I sit here, years later, I gaze at a wall of pictures of the foals that Beau has produced—some of which Bear and I have actually helped welcome into the world. Two of the foals represent a new beginning for the third mare owners, who lost a mare and foal in the fire that horrible winter. They had bred two more mares to Beau, and the result was two healthy, beautiful babies. Of those two, one of them was a beautiful Palomino filly, perfect in every way.

I had written an article for *National Foundation Quarter Horse Association Journal,* which profiled Beau and told of how excited we were anticipating the impending birth of our foal from Charlie. It had been written before we lost her, and it hit the stands about three days after Charlie died. Although it was sad to see it, the brighter side was that we received several calls of interest from people wishing to breed their mares to Beau. We also received calls of encouragement that helped us through an extremely difficult time.

I talk quite a bit about new beginnings, because I feel it's important to realize that, in every aspect of our lives, we are faced with change and adversity. Our lives are full of highs and lows. It is often when we are at our lowest point that we seem to find our greatest strength and our natural ability to survive. Faith plays a big role in this process, as does grief. It's natural to succumb to the grief, as long as we don't allow it to become the controlling factor in our lives. No matter how much we would like to believe that we are in control of fate, when it comes down to it, fate remains in God's hands. We never know what challenges we will face, but whatever hand we're dealt, we must simply play it to the best of our abilities and find the strength to see it through, with no regrets and no looking back; no "what if's" or "if only's."

Only from within can we find the strength to rise again. Despite our loss, we found our new beginning, which was to continue to promote Beau and produce excellent babies. Out of the devastation of losing Charlie, I spent the next five years writing the book *The Foal Is the Goal,* which is dedicated to her.

We think of Charlie often and miss her dearly. We enjoyed her when she was with us, and we remember her fondly. Each horse has a lesson to teach us. Take their lessons and use them well. Every person who touches your life leaves an imprint on your heart. Honor that person by using what you have learned from him or her, and that person will never be forgotten. Face adversity in your life with strength and resolve, and when you need your faith the most, hang on to it as tightly as you can.

Chapter Twelve
Teddy

On Death and Dying

*Y*our life is as long as it is going to be. You do not have complete control over the quantity of your life; however, you can control the quality. I have always believed that a good life far outweighs a long one. When I was growing up, there was a family we knew that mirrored our family. They had the same number of children, who were approximately the same ages as we were. However, there was one difference between that family and ours: We knew very little about loss, and they were experts on the subject. One of their boys was hit by a car and killed out by Mr. Metcalf's barn when he was about 10 years old. One of the girls had complications from an illness and ended up in a coma for years and eventually died. They lost their mother and, eventually, their father and another son. As I said, life is not always fair and equal when it comes to adversity.

Dying is a part of living and it is inevitable, because at some time in our lives, we are all going to die. We have a saying in the horse world: "Life is only as good as your last ride." Our horses teach us to enjoy every day; to live here and now. How well you live each day, how good you are to the people around you, and how much you appreciate each moment of your life—these are the things that are important.

Two weeks ago, I sat on the floor at a friend's house and talked to him while we played cars with his small son. It was a good visit. Yesterday, something snapped in him, and he stabbed his wife, shot one of our deputies and both his children before turning the gun on himself. I struggle with situations such as this because I wonder what in anyone's life could go so wrong that they could ever do such a heinous thing. Regardless of what he had accomplished in his life, he will always be known for that one horrible event.

The way we live our lives affects so many people. Each of us has the ability to change another person's life every day. We are also given the gift of making our own lives better simply by how we perceive our existence. My horses make my life better. They continually enrich me with a sense of calmness and a perspective that allows me to get through the most difficult times in my life. It is an undisputed fact that losing someone or something you love will change you forever. My horse Teddy taught me that, but in his life, he also taught me to laugh and love without reservation. He taught me to be "here and now" and not "there and then." He taught me to appreciate and respect everything and everyone around me. Teddy gave me hope at times when all hope seemed lost. Of all of the stories I share with you, the story of Teddy is by far the most difficult lesson of all. It is the story of a horse who taught me about death and dying, but more importantly, about living life to its fullest. Just as there are special people in our lives whom we'll never forget, there are special horses. Ted E Bear, or Teddy, as we called him, was just such a horse.

After I sold Clarissa, a white Arabian mare, I saved some money to add to the money that I already had and went in search of the perfect horse. A friend, Darrel, who trades horses, had sold a horse that he acquired from Montana—a cow horse that was afraid of cows—to a family with two young girls. The girls were a bit afraid of him, so Darrel decided to sell him again. Darrel thought the horse would be perfect for me.

Teddy wasn't registered; he was a grade horse, so there was no way of knowing where he had actually come from or how many people had owned him over the years. He was about 7 years old—a scruffy, washed-out horse with feathers on his legs that made him resemble a Clydesdale. He was fifteen hands tall and had a long mane and a long tail with thick hair that curled like dreadlocks. Teddy was ugly to most people who saw him, but he had the sweetest eyes I had ever seen. I loved that horse. He had a disposition that told me that he truly loved the company of people.

I remember the day I brought him home. Bear laughed out loud when he saw him. He couldn't believe I had brought him home, much less paid money for him. Nonetheless, there was just something about the horse that drew me to him immediately. If Teddy were a person, he would be a big, dumb jock who would do anything you asked him to do if he trusted you.

The problem was that, although he thrived on affection, when it came to trusting a person in a potentially stressful situation, that trust was tested. He was all right if he was safely within his own space and you just wanted to give him attention. Exposing him to anything outside of his own realm, however, turned him into a scared baby who was sure the world was out to get him. His eyes would get wild and he would immediately flee, just like Clarissa used to do. Yet, unlike Clarissa, once you got him through the initial fear of whatever the obstacle was, he was fine.

There were two exceptions to this rule. One was his fear of balloons. Teddy hated balloons because, while he was at our County Fair one year, a child released a balloon in the barn, and Teddy watched it hover over his stall and then pop above him. The sound echoed through the barn and frightened him. The other was roadkill. He would not walk near roadkill for anything, and he could smell it for miles. He knew when there was roadkill ahead and nothing—I mean absolutely nothing—was going to convince him otherwise.

So, balloons and roadkill would always be Teddy's big fears, but things weren't so simple in the beginning.

I had ridden him in the corral where I bought him, and he was a rock. I took a couple of friends with me, and we decided that under that rough exterior was a good horse that would someday become a *great* horse. After I got him home and Bear stopped laughing at me for buying him, I decided to saddle him up and show Bear how smoothly Teddy rode. It was autumn, so the horseflies were still bad. I got the saddle and bridle in place and picked up a bottle of fly spray from the hitching post and proceeded to spray him. He freaked out and started backing up, not just a few steps but rather the entire thirty or forty feet to the trees. If it's possible for a horse to actually *run* backwards, Teddy was capable of it. I just held on to him and went with him, calmly holding the fly spray until he stopped. Then I would slowly pull the trigger of the sprayer, and we would be off again. Eventually, he overcame that fear and the others that followed.

Bear instantly loved this because Teddy was probably the single greatest challenge that we had ever met. If you would go to hand Teddy an apple, he would immediately assume that it was a bomb that was going to blow him to kingdom come. However, if you took a bite out of the apple first, he would eat it. Bear decided to desensitize him by exposing him to every possible stimulus he could imagine. Bear would come home from work and grab anything he could possibly find. It was the funniest thing I had ever seen. There would be Bear with things like raincoats, blankets, blue plastic tarps, pots and pans, and anything else that may startle a horse. He would spend hours exposing him to everything until, eventually, Teddy wasn't afraid of anything—except of course, the aforementioned balloons and roadkill.

I just wanted to ride my horse, but Bear had Teddy all the time. I would ride him in the daytime when Bear was at work, and when the weekends came, I would get out of bed only to find Bear and Teddy in the woods, clearing trees. Bear had Teddy stand beside him while the trees fell and tied nearby while he ran the chainsaw.

With time, Teddy learned that the trees were not going to land on him. Then Bear would tie the fallen trees to Teddy's saddle horn and teach him to pull logs out of the woods. Teddy eventually paid no mind to chainsaws, power tools, trees falling, or hard work. This is what makes a great horse; investing your time and energy into creating a horse that is versatile in every way.

Teddy would literally eat anything. He had his ration of hay and grain, but if someone had a Mars bar or even a ham sandwich, he was suddenly their best friend. If someone came over with food, Teddy would strike the gate lightly with his front hoof. This attempt to get your attention did not stop until you either let him out so he could follow you around or he got a bite of whatever you had. We had to watch what he ate and drank because as cute as it was, it was fast becoming a major problem.

In all the years we knew Teddy, he never once had a cold, never colicked, and never had any kind of illnesses at all. Once, he ran a nail into his hoof right next to the frog, the soft part on the bottom of the hoof, and was sore for a few days. We soaked it and put him on antibiotics, and he healed nicely. The horse was tough, and we were sure he would outlive us all.

Just as I had hoped, Teddy transformed from an ugly, insecure horse to a priceless companion. His coat eventually turned into a pretty golden color with a completely white mane and a tail that hung to the ground. He was a looker, with a personality that was unsurpassed. Teddy soon became my best friend. He followed me wherever I went, with no lead rope or halter.

We would take him to a show during the day, and several kids would show him in everything from halter and pleasure to barrels and poles. They would place consistently and then that night, we would haul him down to Rising Sun, Ohio, to team pen. We got him over his fear of cows, and he was a riot to take team penning. At home, we would say, "get the dog," and he would go after any dog that moved. The neighbors had two dogs who would chase Bear and Teddy down the road. He was scared of them at first, but Bear turned the situation around and would tell Teddy, "get the dog," and

Teddy would turn and chase the dogs back up the driveway. We used the same principle for chasing the cows, and he caught on immediately. "Get the dog" was his cue to go after one of them. Then he would run and kick up his heels after the time ran out. He was so incredibly fun. I believe that, in order for a horse to do anything well, he has to enjoy whatever he is doing. The same holds true for people. If we find a way to enjoy even the most difficult of tasks, we are happier as a result. Teddy enjoyed everything he did. This horse taught me to love life through his exuberance.

Teddy was excited to go places, and he was ready to get in the trailer and hit the road when we told him we were leaving. We would open the rear door of the trailer, and he would load by himself. He would walk over when he heard the squeaky hinges of the door and get in the trailer. In fact, Teddy used to untie himself as well. We would tie him to the trailer at shows, and he would either come find us or he would go into everyone else's trailer and eat whatever happened to be there. Everyone knew Teddy, so they would usually just tie him back up and give him some hay. I remember sitting in the stands at a show to watch a few classes before it was time for our class and looking down the rail. There was Teddy standing at the rail, watching the show as well. He had untied himself from the trailer and had come to the arena to see what all the excitement was about.

One day, he got into the trailer as he had always done, and we loaded my daughter Jen's horse and headed to Harry Hughes Youth Equestrian Center to work with some of our 4-H kids and their horses. I usually teach the work sessions, so we went early, and I got an opportunity to ride for a while before the kids were ready.

I remember thinking, as I often did, how blessed I was to know such a horse. I can honestly say that I was always appreciative that Teddy was a part of our lives. We were having a wonderful ride, and he was being extremely responsive to my cues. We rode around the arena, and he visited with the kids, who were always excited to see him. I handed him over to Bear, so that he could ride while I worked with the kids and their horses. I didn't know it at the time, but that would be the last time I ever got to know the joy of riding Teddy.

There are days when I think of all the times I had passed on riding him because there were so many more pressing things that needed to be done. In hindsight, I wish I had taken every opportunity to ride and spend time with him and allow those other responsibilities to wait. Life is so precious, and we tend to get wrapped up in what we perceive as important, when the important things are actually the ones that make our lives more enjoyable.

The following day, Teddy nickered as Bear fed him his hay and grain. It was just like any other morning. Bear had let me sleep in because I had started my second novel in the Buckskin mare book series. Ironically enough, I was stuck in a part where I was writing about a horse colicking in south Texas in 1976. I had been e-mailing back and forth with a vet by the name of Greg Bogard, who was helping me with the story line by discussing what was available at the time to help a colicky horse. Colic is severe pain in a horse's digestive tract that causes him to become very ill, and it's often fatal. I was surprised at how few strides had been made in medication and prevention since 1976. I was specifically doing research on a drug called Canadian Bells, which is a mixture of atropine and belladonna. They didn't have banamine then, which is a drug we use now, so they used belladonna instead. They also used to burn the horse's stomach with a spoonful of turpentine to get him to move until the colic passed.

Jen was out of school for the summer, so we both slept late and when we awoke, we did chores. About three o'clock, I went out to talk to Teddy. I chose not to ride him until later because I had promised Jen that we would watch a movie we had rented the day before. Teddy was playing at the fence with Beau, our Palimino Quarter Horse, and everything was all right. After the movie, I decided to ride before we started cooking dinner. It was about five o'clock, and Bear would be home from work soon.

I went to change into my riding clothes and looked out the window. Teddy was down and rolling but he seemed fine, not really thrashing. I went out the back door about ten minutes later, and he was down again. I found that strange, so I whistled to him to see if he would get up. He did and then immediately went down again. I hollered to Jen, "Come quick, something's wrong with Teddy." She laughed because nothing was ever wrong with him—he was a rock. She ran outside, and as I ran for the barn to get to the closest phone, I heard her scream. I looked, and, apparently, he had risen, walked over to her and nickered, and then just dropped at her feet. I went to Teddy and told Jen to call the vet. It was a clear case of colic from the way he was acting. A horse person knows colic by obvious signs such as sweating, heavy breathing, and an inability to find a comfortable position. They lie down, get up, paw the ground, lie down again, and roll. At times, they moan and repeat the process.

I knew I had to get some banamine in him, but I also had to stop him from rolling. I got him to his feet and managed to get him to the round pen, where I could walk him. Thank goodness Bear pulled in the driveway just then and helped me keep him on his feet. Jen had called our vet, Roger, and then came out to help us.

As the situation worsened, aside from Bear and Jen, our neighbors and two of our clients were there. Roger had one of his Thoroughbreds get loose from the barn as he was leaving, but he still arrived in record time. We all tried to get Teddy back on his feet, but he was determined to lie down. We gave him banamine and Ace Bromine to calm him and prevent him from thrashing. When things seemed under control, Roger left after giving us instructions to call him if he got any worse. He lives only a short distance away and could travel back, if necessary.

Things were all right for a short period of time, and then worsened again. I called Roger to give him an update on Teddy's condition. Everyone took turns walking Teddy, but it was clear he was slipping fast. He was extremely restless and still in a lot of pain. I told Roger that we had decided to take him to Findlay College's Equine Emergency Services.

By seven o'clock, we had him loaded in the trailer and made the hour-long drive to Findlay. It was an hour that felt like an eternity, and Bear and I barely spoke for the entire trip because we were so scared that we might lose him. Teddy didn't lie down once, and he called

My siblings and I enjoying a break in a neighbor's pool. This was taken around the time I met Dewey.

Mom (Katy) in Katy's House Of Kurls, dressed up as Dale Evans for Halloween.

Some children and I hoping to get a chance to ride. I'm on the far right. This was taken right around the time my siblings and I were trading labor for rides at Mr. Metcalf's.

My husband, Bear, taking a photo of one of our many babies. Apparently she's ready for her close-up.

Beau and I with our ribbon just minutes after placing in the top five stallions in the world at the Palomino Horse Breeders Association World Championship Show in Tulsa, Oklahoma.

Joker saddled up and ready to go.

Teddy was the love of my life.

My youngest daughter, Jennifer, with her pony, Checkers, at the Fulton County Fair in Wauseon, Ohio.

Braving the elements for a trail ride with a guest at our ranch in Ohio.
Riding Teddy (left) and Magic (right) through the snow.

My dad, whom I lovingly call
Pawdaddy, first taught me the love
of horses. This is him riding one of
the many horses he knew.

My friend Kelly Kothmann's ranch in Junction, Texas. This is where
I rode the Mexican pony and learned to rope.

Dakota was a
beautiful horse with
a heart of gold.

Sparky and sibling, just two of Beau's many babies, pictured at Hollowbrook Farm in Danville, Vermont.

One of the babies by Cher, one of two mares from Texas.

Cher and her sister Robin, the Texas Mares, both have the G brand on their hindquarters.

Hootie, who taught me about survival and strength, curled up for a long nap. He was just days old here.

from the trailer. Roger had called the vet at Findlay, so he knew we were on our way, and he was ready for us when we got there.

We had always been told that if you take a horse with colic to the college, you had better walk in with at least $2,000. There we were with every credit card we could get our hands on, even some from other people, such as Bear's mom and the friends who were helping us.

Teddy's heart rate was still high, which told us that even after all the medication we had given him, he was still in a lot of pain. The doctors gave him more medication, and we waited as they ran tests and found nothing. Surgery was not an option with his heart rate so high. He was slipping fast. We continued to walk him, but his head was down with his nose touching the floor. The vet pulled me aside, and I immediately asked him what we were going to do. I didn't envy the vets—here I am standing there with all my credit cards begging them to save this horse. The vet said that Teddy's chance of surviving surgery where slim to none due to his heart rate and advanced symptoms. The veterinary assistant explained to me what an enterolith was, and how calcium can form around the smallest piece of grain, wood, or anything in a horse's digestive tract, which could, in turn, cause blockage that a vet can't necessarily feel upon an initial exam. The fact that he had never been sick was suddenly not such a great thing after all because apparently he had no tolerance for the pain he was experiencing. He kept trying to lie down, and it was getting more and more difficult to get him up.

Jeff, one of the vets, told me that it was time to make a decision. I asked him if Teddy were his horse, what he would do. He said he didn't like giving odds and he didn't like to make decisions for other people, but if it were his horse, he would find the grace to let him go quietly. It had been three hours and there was no change. Teddy's beautiful amber eyes were now blue and hazy. When I walked over and took him from Bear, Teddy didn't even realize I was there. He was dying and I had to find the strength to let him go. Not one person in the room that night could make the decision for me—not the vet who had been so honest with me about where we stood, not the technicians who had tried in vain to save him, not even Bear who knew how much I loved that horse.

At that moment, I thought about the killer pens and how sad those horses were. I wondered if each of their people had not had the courage to face this type of decision, so instead, they chose a different route. The killing of horses used for the consumption of meat is such a controversial subject among horse people, and yet to ban the practice could create so many situations where a sick or dying horse may suffer even more due to lack of options.

I believe that in our lives, when people hurt us or disappoint us, we build imaginary walls around ourselves for protection. These walls also seclude us from the outside world. I had spent my life building a fortress of such emotional walls. After years of moving around and being forced to make new friends and starting over once or twice a year, it had become easy for me to build walls in an attempt to protect myself from the disappointment of having to move again and leave friends behind. It had become easier to hide behind the emotional walls than to step up and take a chance that the people I came to love would be in my life for longer than a year or so.

Horses do not care about anything beyond the love of the people they meet. They are not judgmental, nor in any way prejudiced. They want simply to be your friend. Now here was this animal who never saw any of those walls, who loved me unconditionally and wanted very little in return. I trusted this horse, and he eventually bestowed that trust upon me. When I needed him, he was always there. He taught me how to open up and love without reservation. Teddy was such a part of who I was and to give him up, I would be forced to give up a large part of myself.

Yet, here he was, dying in front of me. For the first time, he needed me to be there for him, and I knew I had to find the strength to let him go. Every instinct I had told me that the horse I loved was already so far gone that it was time to allow him an escape from this unbearable pain. They had tried everything they could, and it was killing me to see him struggle, to watch him die a painful death right before my eyes. When I hugged his thick beautiful neck, he didn't even flinch, there was no response. It pained me to listen to the shallow breathing of an animal in such excruciating pain. I buried my face in his long white mane and cried. I prayed to God to give me the strength to do the right thing for Teddy, and the barn fell silent as I said goodbye to this amazing creature.

I handed the lead rope over to Jeff, who reassured me that I had made the only decision that I could possibly make. As I let go of him, every second that I had spent with him came flooding back to me like a painful reminder of what I was about to walk away from; every moment of every day that I had known this beautiful horse now hurt beyond belief. I did not look back as I walked outside to the trailer. Every step of the way I wanted nothing more than to turn around and look at him one more time. I can't begin to describe how badly it hurt to walk away. In my head, I knew that it was the right decision, that the most unselfish thing I could do was to let him go. In my heart, I knew that if I turned around to see him one more time, I would not have the strength to let him go.

I could feel Bear's presence behind me, but he didn't say a word. He was now trying desperately to put his own feelings aside. He just let me know that he was there. Later, I understood how helpless he felt watching me as I cried harder than I ever had. He had experienced that grief once before with Charlie and he knew that I had to find the strength within myself. Nothing he could say would make any difference at all.

In June of his eighth year with us, we lost Teddy to colic. While he gave us so much in his life, there is even something to be learned in his death. It's a lesson of new beginnings and missed opportunities, of breaking down walls, of how the love of a horse can break down those barriers that people just can't seem to get through.

Teddy was a rare and special gift that taught me the pure and simple fact that losing someone you love will change you forever. A loved one's death is the single greatest challenge you will ever face, and being put in a situation where you have to make the decision between their own comfort and the pain of losing them is more difficult than any decision you will ever have to make.

I had been given the privilege of knowing a really good horse for eight years, and although it was painful to lose him, the moments we spent together were priceless. Teddy had taught us the importance of communicating mutual trust. He taught us that persistence and patience are two very valuable tools needed to get past challenges and find the good horse that lies within. Teddy taught me that when letting go of a loved one, strength is the most important tool that you can possess. I also learned that the love stays with you, and the memories of the person or horse that you love are yours to keep.

My faith allows me the privilege of believing that Teddy is now in a wonderful place, free of pain, and eternally happy. The events of that night will forever remain with me. Teddy brought joy to my life, my family's life, and to the lives of all of the people that knew and loved him. Life is about quality, not quantity; Teddy taught me that. He taught me that the only thing that matters is how well we live our lives here and now. Live every day as though it was your last ride, and you will have no regrets.

Chapter Thirteen
Checkers

Children and Competition

*C*hildren and competition is a very controversial subject of late. We have all heard horror stories about soccer dads and cheerleader moms getting a little out of control on behalf of their children. We have to remember that kids want to play; they want to go out there in any sport and just have fun. Although we want them to be successful in their ventures, we must allow them to be children and play instead of taking something too seriously.

Bear and I decided that, because our daughter Jennifer had shown Teddy as her 4-H project for the first year, it was time for her to have a horse of her own who could take her to higher levels. We wanted her to have a horse who could teach her the joy of winning but not necessarily one who would do it all for her. We still wanted her to have to work hard to do well, but an older, more experienced horse was what she needed to give her the confidence to advance her skills. The pleasure of my first ride on such a horse was incredibly exciting for me, because Dewey took care of me enough that I could just have fun. Jen needed a Dewey horse in her life.

We had heard about a gentleman in Indiana who always had a herd of horses for sale. One Sunday, we took the day to drive over and see what he had. When we arrived, he and his son were waiting outside for us, and they had about five or six horses already saddled, bridled, and tied up to the rails of a fence.

An honest seller will want you to be happy with your horse and, therefore, will do his best to match the horse and rider, even if this means he doesn't have a match in his own herd. However, the seller can help only if you tell him what you want, so communication is very important! The person who owns the horse also needs to be experienced and able to understand both horse and rider personalities.

A good first step is to make sure the seller is trustworthy. I try to buy horses from people through referrals so that I know something about the seller before I look at the horse. I also ask a lot of questions about the prospective horse; as the buyer, I try to find out as much as possible about the horse I am considering. We explained to the seller exactly what type of horse we wanted; the main points I made clear were Jen's riding level and how the horse would be used.

The fact that the horses were already saddled and bridled may have saved us time, but I prefer arriving in time to see the horse's manners when handled and saddled. It gives me better insight into what the horse is like. It is important not only that I see the horse without tack when I am looking to buy, but also that I am able to see the horse's responses when being tacked. For instance, if the owner were to cinch the saddle, would the horse turn and pin his ears or back up? Or, would he stand quietly? This was a very important issue to us because Jennifer was the one who would be tacking up the horse, and she was only 10 years old.

We told Jen that we would ride the horses first, and then she would watch and narrow it down to a couple that she would like to ride. When I go to buy a horse, I always have the owner of the horse ride first. Not only can I learn about the horse through observation, but I also don't want to buy a horse that the owner won't even ride.

I asked the seller's son, Jason, to ride a little bay mare that Jen liked. I asked him to have her walk, trot, canter, stop, and back so that I could see how well she moved. I also wanted to know whether she was nervous, stressed, or irritated when asked to perform simple tasks. If Jen was going to work this mare, we would need the mare to be willing. Getting her involved in every aspect of finding her next horse would help Jen continue to improve and stay interested in her chosen sport. Respecting your child's opinion is of the utmost importance.

While Jason rode her, Jen and I discussed whether or not this mare was far enough along for her. She decided that the mare wasn't, because Jen was looking for a horse who knew a little more of what was required for the show ring. This mare was older, and it would take too much time to get her ready. This mare also got frustrated when Jason asked her to pick up a canter. She would repeatedly pin her ears, spin her tail, and trot faster. We thanked him and asked him if he would ride another horse instead. When he removed the saddle, we noticed that she had a large scar on her back that the saddle pad had hidden.

When we walked back to the pen where the other horses were tied, we found Bear riding a horse that was bucking. We laughed as we heard the seller yell, "Just hold on, he'll stop any time." He didn't. The horse bucked Bear all the way down the driveway and back again. This was definitely not the horse for Jen.

After we witnessed this rodeo, we explained once again to the man and his son that we were looking for a kid-safe horse that had been shown before and therefore would have at least a little bit of show-ring manners. He was honest enough to tell us that neither of them showed horses and that this particular group of horses had been brought in just a few days earlier and were fairly green. We thanked them both for their time and left. It was disappointing to leave without a horse, but we knew better than to settle for an inappropriate horse. It was Jen's decision, and she needed to find a horse who would allow her to accomplish what she wanted to do.

We spent the following week calling on almost every horse in the newspaper and every horse we heard about from friends. We came across an ad for a pony, and although Jen didn't want a pony, this particular one was just a few inches shorter than a horse. The young girl who had owned her had shown her extensively. Jen was happy to see that the mare didn't look like a typical pony—short and squatty—but was instead a small horse. In fact, she was put together exceptionally well.

She was a Sorrel Paint, with three white socks and a white spot on her side in the shape of the state of Florida. The girl had owned her for several years and named her Mei Paycheque because she had saved every paycheck she made to buy her. Her barn name was Checkers. The mare acted like a princess who expected everyone to comply with her every wish. She watched me out of the corner of her eye skeptically. The mare absolutely could not tolerate small children running around her. She actually threatened to nip at them, and pinned her ears when they got close. But despite her snootiness, this mare positively loved Jennifer.

From the moment they met, it was as though they had known each other all their lives. There was just one small problem. When we met Checkers, she was already in her early twenties, and we knew that the average horse lived approximately twenty-five years or so. We were so afraid that Jennifer would get attached to her and she would die or that she would have all kinds of medical problems and become unrideable. We discussed all this with Jen and she understood, but still wanted the mare. Although we were wary of her age, safety was our first consideration, and this little mare loved Jen. She took care to lower her head so Jen could put the bridle in place and stood perfectly still while she placed the saddle on her back. I watched as Jen squealed with delight when she rode her. It took me back to that day with Dewey, and I just knew Checkers and Jen would be a match made in heaven.

We immediately went to work with her, and by July, Jennifer had qualified for the State Fair in Columbus, Ohio. This was the biggest show Jen had ever attended, and it would require us to be there two days and two nights. Because Jen was only 10 years old, we weren't sure whether she was ready for this level of competition. We told Jen that at any time, if she decided that competing wasn't for her, we would go home.

By the time State Fair arrived, Jen had ridden Checkers so much that when she heard the announcer give the instructions to walk, jog, or lope, the horse would follow the instructions before Jen even had a chance to cue her. We used to tease her that she should sit in the audience and let Checkers do the class without her.

There were thirty-two kids in her showmanship class and about as many in her horsemanship class. It was at least 95 degrees in the arena, and I prayed that the mare wouldn't drop dead from a combination of old age and heat exhaustion. Showmanship was first, and although Jen and Checkers didn't place, they both did fine. Horsemanship came next, and in spite of the fact that Jen was one of four who did the pattern perfectly, the judge didn't place her.

Jen was very disappointed, but we were lucky enough to have a judge who was willing to answer questions. He told her that he disqualified her for talking to a friend of hers on the rail during the class. He said that he felt this showed a lack of respect. He was right, and respect was an important lesson for Jen to learn. Upon leaving the fairgrounds, everyone was a little blue because she didn't come home with any ribbons. The blues wore off quickly, though, as we realized how much fun the whole experience was. It taught Jen more about showing, and it gave her an opportunity to spend more time with her horse. Jen truly regretted her actions in the ring; she commented that she never wanted to show under that judge again because she was so embarrassed. Jen learned her lesson and never made the same mistake again.

A little over a month later, Jen took Checkers to our County Fair. She was extremely excited to show, camp, and be with her horse and horse friends for an entire week. The morning of the Junior Fair show came, and Jen panicked. There, in the arena, was the same judge who had disqualified her at the State Fair. Although she was sure he would remember her and not place her because of the incident at State, she rode well and won the title of Grand Champion Pleasure Pony. In fact, she did well in all her classes and more importantly, she had fun. He was a very fair judge and rewarded her for her hard work.

Even though Checkers was going strong in the show ring, she had developed an eye irritation that clogged her tear ducts repeatedly and required periodic flushing. She needed eye drops administered daily, and also seemed to be developing some arthritis. Just as we had dreaded, her age was beginning to catch up with her. The winter found her struggling to stay warm, so every day, Jen blanketed her and gave her warm water to drink. The arrival of spring made it easier for Checkers to cope with the challenges of getting old, but she simply couldn't keep up with Jen's level of activity. We decided that Checkers would be better off with a family who would love her, but would ride and show her only occasionally.

Jen learned so much about showing by spending time with such an experienced horse. I hear of too many people who want to buy a young horse for their child so that the two can "grow up together." It has been our experience that someone has to be the teacher. Jen never would have experienced the thrill of competition and success had she chosen a less experienced horse. It was through Checkers that she gained the confidence and experience she needed to excel in the horse industry.

When we made the decision to sell Checkers, we let Jen meet the prospective buyers and show them the horse. By having Jen talk about Checker's likes and dislikes, we hoped she would become comfortable with the family who would buy her. Getting our child involved in every aspect of horse care was extremely important to us. It not only teaches children to be caring and responsible, but also creates caring and responsible adults. In the case of Checkers, we wanted Jennifer to feel good about where her friend was going so that she wouldn't miss her so much and wonder whether her owners were caring for her.

Several people showed up to see Checkers, and Jen would rule out each and every one of them. We were beginning to think that she was never going to sell her at all. Finally, Jen was convinced that the "right" people had come to see her, and she allowed Checkers to leave. We sold her for exactly what we had paid for her.

Checkers spent only one year with her new family. She died the following winter. Although it hurt very much to hear the news, Jen knew that Checkers had lived a long and happy life with loving, caring people, right up to the end.

The fine line between competition and having fun should be balanced carefully. There has to be a genuine interest in the sport and a certain level of maturity on the part of the child as well as the parents. Be involved in sports and encourage your children to compete, but don't get so involved that it loses its appeal for the children. Stand on the sidelines and cheer them on and be proud of them, but don't interfere with their love of the game and their need to just have fun.

Never try to live out your dreams through your children; allow them to live their own dreams. Never allow it to be about the ribbons or the rewards, but rather about the thrill of the competition. As people who have nurtured children through a love of horses for many years, we have seen children who are put under such pressure that they actually throw up before a class or leave a class in tears. We have seen parents place their children in harm's way for the sake of winning, and we have watched these children grow up to hate horses as a result. When Jennifer turned 17, she asked if she could sell her horse to buy her first car, and of course we told her yes. She is 22 now and has ridden many horses over the years, and she fondly remembers every one.

Chapter Fourteen
Magic

Discovering Pure Joy

*L*ooking for pure, unadulterated joy in your life can be difficult, but it is so important. To laugh out loud and feel the way you did when you were a child is one of life's greatest pleasures. Most of my memories involving my kids and horses are of our youngest daughter, Jennifer, because of her dedicated and lasting involvement with horses. Our oldest daughter, Dusty, found enjoyment in other hobbies and interests. Today, Dusty is 28 and in college. She has a 6-year-old son named Garrett who is the funniest human being I know. He loves the horses. I can only hope that the horse genes that skipped Dusty are passed on to Garrett. I say this half-jokingly, because I know some people are horse people, and some are not.

I realized when Garrett was 4 that he had a definite interest when I turned my back on him for a split second while cleaning stalls and found him sitting in the pasture with the horses. My first instinct was to panic because he was sitting on the ground with two mares and their babies, talking to them and showing them his truck. He had their undivided attention! Then I realized that if I panicked,

I would be instilling fear in him that seemed unnecessary. I calmly went in with him and reminded him that he was not allowed to be in with the horses without me.

"Why?" he asked. I hesitated for a moment and replied, "Because one of them might hurt you."

He laughed. "Don't be silly Nana, look at them; they like me." I couldn't argue with that, they definitely liked him. "These horses will never hurt me," he added.

Being the only small child on a horse ranch, he had made friends with the horses, and although we watched him as much as we could, we continuously found him in the barn every chance he got to sneak away. At 6 years old, Garrett spends his evenings riding his bike up and down the center aisle in the barn, chatting with the horses. He has his favorites, and yet when it came time to choose a horse for him, he surprised all of us. Bear and I were going to get him a pony, and instead, he wanted a sixteen-hand black racing stallion named Guidance System. I put my foot down, and he decided he wanted a lamb instead. Go figure.

It can be difficult to take an objective view as to whether or not your children are interested enough in horses to do the work that is involved in caring for a horse. Sometimes we want so badly for our kids to love horses—or any sport for that matter—that we just assume it to be true, even if the child has no interest. We have always told both of the girls that if their interests lie elsewhere, they should pursue what makes them happy.

I can't stress enough the importance of listening to your children and believing them when they say that they are just not interested. We can't live our lives through our kids without some damage to their own identity.

Dusty has never shown a horse, not even at a fun show, and has no desire to do so. In fact, three months after we built the larger barn, she came in looking for me to tell me that I had a phone call and was surprised at the fact that there were actually stalls. She had no reason to go out there because its progress didn't affect her in any way. She did, however, learn during her high school years that horses make great "guy bait." Plain and simple, if a wannabe cowboy knows you have horses, he wants to come over to your house.

This is where Magic comes in. One winter, Bear surprised me with a new horse. The guy delivered him to our barn on the afternoon of Christmas Eve. Magic was a paint horse, and from the first day he arrived, I knew exactly what his human personality was; he was a troublemaker. He knew the secrets of escaping and used them quite often. When teamed up with Teddy's playful personality, our other horse at the time, the two of them were like partners in crime.

Magic had the most incredible lope, and he could do flying lead changes at the drop of a hat. He was fast, and he would dig in when we ran. He knew his business, but when he wanted to be a punk, he would just throw away everything he had learned and goof off. If you entertained or encouraged this behavior in him, he would goof off even more. Magic was like that person you know who wasn't always trustworthy but could make you laugh until your sides hurt.

Dusty had just met Shawnee, the star football player and possibly the most popular kid at school. He was a wannabe cowboy. When he heard that we had horses, he immediately invited himself over to go riding. One morning, we woke to find six inches of fresh snow and a broken gate. Magic and Teddy were gone. Dusty called Shawnee, who lived behind our woods, and he came over to help search for them. We followed the tracks through yards, under swing sets, up to people's windows, in small circles that led to larger circles that finally led to one hundred acres of unplanted open field. That's where we found the two of them foraging for any grass they could find. It was very early in the morning, and the sun hadn't completely risen yet. Bear and Shawnee approached them, and being the little gang that the two horses were, the chase was on.

Bear and Shawnee circled the two horses back to the barn and finally lured them back to their stalls with some grain. Bear and Shawnee became fast friends after an hour of trekking through the snow in the dark, chasing horses. He started to come over to ride, and it was humorous watching Dusty, who had never shown an interest in the horses, bluff her way through his endless questions about them. What was funnier yet was to watch her meet him at the barn in my oversized cowboy boots, attempting to fit in.

Shawnee loved Teddy, which left Dusty to ride Magic. Don't get me wrong, Magic was a great horse in the sense that he had speed and athleticism and he was so much fun to ride, but he had a wild streak a mile wide. This horse lived to run. Dusty hopped on Magic and Shawnee hopped on Teddy, and they set off along the trails. Dusty bluffed her way through Shawnee's endless questions pretty well until they were about a mile or so from the house. According to Shawnee, who laughed as he ponied Magic back to the barn while Dusty limped home covered in mud and leaves, they had picked up a canter and Magic thought it was a race. He took off at a dead run, and Dusty fell off. Shawnee then caught him, and they returned home. Dusty insisted that she would rather walk back. That night after Shawnee left to go home, Dusty asked if I could give her some lessons on Teddy so that she could learn how to ride. She promised me that her newfound interest in the horses had nothing to do with Shawnee. I suspected otherwise.

I got her up at the crack of dawn. I had her ride bareback to build up her leg muscles and really demonstrate her desire to ride. I explained that there was more to it than just riding. I had her clean stalls, drag arenas, scrub water buckets, and do all the other usual chores that go with having a genuine interest in horses. The next day, we were supposed to meet at the barn for her second lesson and she slept in, telling me that she was too sore to ride. She decided that horses just weren't worth the effort.

As for Shawnee, he bought a pair of spurs that I personally would never wear to ride a horse unless I had a death wish. They had pointed rowels that were about as big around as a silver dollar, and he loved them because they jingled when he walked. Magic, on the other hand, hated them. I tried to explain to Shawnee that wearing those spurs was not a good idea. Despite my advice, he was determined to try them out.

Shawnee and several of Dusty's other friends showed up at the barn. I looked out to see them standing on the rail of our large arena.

Although it was mostly empty, it still hadn't been completely cleared of trees. Magic and Teddy were grazing peacefully and pretty much minding their own business. I watched in disbelief as Shawnee caught Magic and attached a lead rope to his halter. He swung up on to his back and turned him to face the other end of the arena. The minute those wannabe cowboy spurs hit his sides, the pleasure of the ride was finished for Shawnee. Magic bucked all the way to the other end of the 120-foot arena. I was impressed that Shawnee managed to stay on for a few seconds; every time Magic's head came up, Shawnee would try to hold on, only to accidentally spur Magic again, causing Magic to buck some more. Shawnee bailed off as they hit the trees. I am glad he came away with only his pride bruised. I never saw those spurs again.

From that point on, Shawnee learned to respect the advice people gave him about horses. He also became a much more cautious rider. I still wear my black Charlie One Horse hat that he gave me when his interest turned to motorcycles. Every time I hear a pair of spurs jingling, I think of Shawnee and remember that summer.

After the incident with Shawnee, Magic earned a reputation of being a renegade horse. It was not deserved in this instance, as it was merely a case of someone pretending to know more than he really did. Magic was not a horse that you could ever drop your guard with, but certainly not a renegade. In our experience, people create renegade horses. Magic was one of those horses that took full advantage of all situations. He would test and retest his riders to see whether he could get away with anything more. That aside, this horse was nothing short of pure, unadulterated joy. He was the bad boy that you hung out with just for the fun of it. He was the one friend that your mother hated, so you spent as much time with him as possible.

Magic taught me that when I needed an escape, I could grab him and take off for a run through the fields behind our farm, and I would always feel better when I came home. Why do you think this horse's name was Magic? He was better than any therapy—one hour with him on a winding trail at a full run was more therapy than years of lying on a psychiatrist's couch, telling him your problems. Magic provided the ultimate escape from life, worries, and anything bad that happened to creep up on any given day.

I think we all need that in our lives sometimes; it's important. Be responsible in your life and work hard, but every now and again, escape! Be spontaneous and book a cruise at the last minute or get on a plane or just drive until you find a place that makes you happy and lets you just "be" for a while. Discover whatever it is that would be the perfect escape and do it. No one is going to ever give you that time; you have to give it to yourself. For a day, a week, or even just a couple of hours, do something that is exciting and takes your breath away. You will find that you will come back refreshed and better equipped to face the challenges of life.

Horses listen without judgment, and their goal in life is to have fun. Learn this lesson from them above all else and do not feel guilty. You are no good to anyone unless you are good to yourself first.

Chapter Fifteen
Osado

Pride

*H*orses have excellent instincts. Some have a very distinct dislike for certain people. Sometimes we realize why they dislike a person the moment we meet that person. Other times, we find out much later and realize that we should have trusted the horse's instincts and just stayed away. That is not to say that horses are always right. However, it has been my experience that, for the most part, their instincts are pretty reliable.

For example, I remember an intuitive little horse that I borrowed to go on a trail ride. I was on a poker run in a nearby park. A *poker run* is a creative poker game in which you must stop at various checkpoints and draw a card from the person who mans the station. All riders then compare poker hands when the trail ride is over. The horse I was riding bolted through the trees with me just to avoid a rather quiet gentleman who was handing out cards. I later met the man for the first time and noticed needle marks up and down his arms. I can't say for sure whether he was a drug addict or had a medical condition, but they were certainly needle marks. All I know is that there was no way this horse was going near him.

One day, I got a call from a woman, Rae, whom I had known for years. She is probably one of the sweetest women I have ever met. She always had a kind word to say about everyone. She genuinely cared about others' feelings and would give you her last dollar if she thought you needed it. It seemed Rae had a problem. She had purchased a gelding at an auction after someone she trusted encouraged her to buy it. Once the horse was in her barn, he began to act aggressive, pinning his ears and baring his teeth whenever she approached. She was afraid of the horse, and for good reason.

She wanted me to work with the horse for thirty days. She had purchased him with the intention of showing him, and either he had to respect her or she would have to sell him. Either way, the bad habit needed to be fixed. I agreed to take him for thirty days and show him in a local show before I sent him back. When Osado arrived, we all expected him to be uncontrollable because of the things we had heard about him. Instead, the horse we met was a sweetheart. He was about sixteen hands tall, maybe taller, and had such a presence about him that could only be described as noble. He wasn't aggressive at all; in fact, he warmed up to us almost immediately.

The more we worked with him, the better he became. He had been a stallion and was gelded only recently, so this could have been a source of his aggressiveness. However, to us, he was a pussycat. I rode him every day and taught him to *square up* (stand as expected) and *pivot* (turn on his hind leg) for the Halter and Showmanship classes. Bear worked with him as well, and both of us *longed* him (taught him movement while handling him on a long lead line) and worked on *ground manners* (good behavior while on lead). We were very proud of how he was coming along and were anxious for Rae to see the results.

Usually, when we are working with someone else's horse, we have that person over at least two or three times to keep her abreast of the horse's progress and teach her how to ask the horse to do various things. This was not true in Osado's case. As per the owner's request, it would just be the horse and us without any outside distractions until he was show ready. I finally called Rae to tell her that we would be taking Osado to a show the following weekend. Unfortunately, she wasn't able to attend, but she trusted our judgment and would be over to the barn the following day to make the decision as to whether or not she would sell him.

The following Monday, I broke my ribs while riding another horse that I was working, and Bear took up the slack with Osado for the week before the show. Bear had no interest in showing, but I had promised Rae that I would show Osado. I felt obligated. Against all common sense, and with Bear's absolute disapproval, I taped my ribs tightly, got dressed, and rode into the arena on Osado. It was busier than we had hoped; there were twenty-four people in my class.

Although Osado was a little nervous about the crowd, he was doing all right. I was as well, until we got to a corner where a girl was having a problem with her horse. Just as I tried to pass her, her horse backed up and slammed into Osado. He went backward about three steps and reared. I could feel my ribs punishing me for my poor decision to ride. I got Osado back under control, and we rode once more around the arena. The announcer called for us to line up in the middle of the ring for the placing. It seemed like we stood for an eternity, and I began to have trouble breathing. I spotted Bear on the rail, glaring at me in anger. As soon as the judge excused us, he met me at the rail and took the horse. He sarcastically asked me whether I was done yet, and I told him that I was.

I vividly remember sitting in the truck cutting the tape off of my ribs and trying not to cry; it hurt so badly. Because it was important to Rae that we assess the horse fairly so she could make a decision, I abandoned my common sense. I paid dearly for that.

Regardless of the situation, Osado did well. Other than his reaction to the horse acting up, we had a nice ride. He wasn't at all aggressive with the other horses. That night, I called Rae and told her about the show. She decided that it was time to visit Osado and make a decision.

Rae came over the next day. The sorrow on her face when she walked in the barn simply broke my heart. She approached his stall, and he immediately pinned his ears and bared his teeth. This was the first time in the thirty days since his arrival that he had showed such aggression, and it surprised me. Rae walked out of the barn and told us to sell him. I could see the tears in her eyes. For no apparent reason, this horse hated her, and to this day, I will never understand why. Once she left, he settled right down and began munching on his hay. I walked over to the stall, and he greeted me with the utmost respect.

She made a good decision; she and the horse just didn't see eye to eye. She gave him every chance, and he still didn't like her. I respected her decision. She knew she wasn't comfortable, so instead of aggravating the situation or risking injury, she walked away. She did not allow her pride to get in the way of a relationship. She tried everything that she could to get the horse to like her to no avail, so she walked away.

There are people you meet who are going to clash with your own personality. Others will not like you for whatever reason. Never take this personally, because it could have little to do with you at all. It could be that someone is simply having a bad day. It is possible that you may meet again under other circumstances, and it will be different. Pride is a foolish and useless emotion when dealing with people. However, what Osado teaches us here is as much about instinct as anything else. Your instinct will protect you from trusting the wrong people. For instance, if you are getting in your car and a stranger approaches you in a parking lot, your instinct immediately tells you that you are not safe. Trust that instinct. Even if it is based on absolutely nothing, as Osado's seemed to be with Rae, trust it. You will be much safer trusting your instinct and being wrong than ignoring it and being right. I know that Rae is no longer involved with horses and, honestly, I never see her anymore at all. It is as though she just disappeared one day.

Two people came to see Osado before he was sold. The woman who bought Osado was petite and sweet and reminded me of Rae. He took an immediate liking to her, and, as far as we know, she still has him.

Chapter Sixteen
Breezy

Sharing Your Passion with Others

haring your passion with others is an excellent way to find something in common with those you love. However, if those you love don't share that particular passion, the results can be disastrous.

I swore never again to buy an Arabian horse after Clarissa. I don't consider Arabians a breed to avoid or feel they aren't intelligent, because they certainly are. They are also quite possibly the most breathtakingly beautiful breed of horse. I didn't want another Arab because I had decided that I simply did not have the temperament for them. I believed there was a horse for every personality, and my preference leaned more toward the mild manners of the Quarter Horse. Breezy changed my mind about that.

Jim was a friend who was a paraplegic; a horrible automobile accident had left him in a wheelchair. Although he'd had horses as a young man, it had been a few years since he had ridden, and he dearly missed their company. He had purchased several horses for his family, but they eventually lost interest. He asked Bear and me to come over and take a look at the horses. He wanted to sell them all and get out of horses completely. He didn't have a choice in the matter; his health was getting worse, and the horses were not being cared for properly. He was bedridden, so he had not personally been out to the barn in quite a while. Instead, he had hired two young boys to care for the horses and paid them well for their services.

When we arrived, the horses were turned out. We could see two Arabian babies, a Morgan baby, and from a distance, what looked to be a Quarter Horse mare, all standing at the rail watching us. The mare was in a large pasture all by herself and when we approached, she nickered to us softly. Upon closer inspection, we could see that she had a Quarter Horse–type body, but her features were very refined. Her head was beautifully proportioned, and her face was *dished*—flat with a slight inward curve to her profile, a typical Arabian trait. She was a beautiful chestnut color with eyes that were large and sweet. Her Arabian influence could not be denied.

We encouraged her to move around the pasture so that we could see her way of going, but at first she just wanted to be near us. Once she moved freely around the vast, open pasture, her tail went up, and she pranced from where we stood to the opposite end of the pasture and back again. It was as though she were floating on air. She was quick, and yet her stride was consistent with turns that were extremely well orchestrated. Although her coat was dull and her eyes were not very bright, she was majestic. After watching her move gracefully out across the pasture, I understood why she was named Breezy. We left her for the time being in order to have a closer look at the younger horses. She watched us from the nearest corner of her pasture the entire time we were there.

The babies were thin and looked as though they hadn't gotten any attention in a long time. When Jim had called us that morning, Bear and I were visiting with some friends, a woman and her husband, and they were interested in buying a horse, so they came along to see what Jim had. The friend immediately liked the Arabian colt and expressed an interest in buying him. Her husband liked the other Arabian baby, so we made them a deal on the two horses on Jim's behalf. We knew they would have excellent care.

I went in the house and spoke to Jim about the horses. He was extremely saddened at their condition, so I downplayed their neglect to spare his feelings. He had had a feeling, from the comments a few people had made, that the horses were not being cared for properly. This is why he wanted us to sell them.

He asked about the Morgan colt in the barn, which surprised me—I hadn't even thought to look in the barn, since the other Morgan baby, Breezy, and the two Arabian babies were outside when we arrived. We had overlooked one horse and honestly, had Jim not mentioned him, we may have left the poor guy behind. He trusted us to find all of them good homes.

After I finished visiting with Jim, Bear and I went to the barn to see the little Morgan. A young man who worked at the barn, and had obviously taken advantage of Jim by neglecting the horses, led us there. He took us to a dark, filthy stall. There was an overhead light with a broken bulb and shards of glass all over the stall floor. The young horse stood in a corner, which made it extremely difficult for us to see him. I asked the boy whether he could bring the horse out in the light of the hallway. He did. The baby was so skinny and so wormy that he could barely stand. He staggered and fell down in the hallway. The boy informed us, in his infinite wisdom, that he thought the horse was dying. It was obvious that the boy didn't know that he was at least partially responsible for the horse's condition, so we gave him the benefit of the doubt and said nothing to place blame.

Leaving the foal there to die was not a consideration. We also knew that he was too weak to be moved. Bear told the boy that we would leave the horse behind, and that he was to meet the vet for shots and worming. We would pay him to clean the stall and feed and water the horse *regularly* until we could get him strong enough to haul him home. The boy protested at first, but Bear told him that he should be ashamed of himself for the way he had cared for these horses, and that we would be by every day to check on the foal. The boy agreed without argument. There was one more thing to which we made him agree: He was not, under any circumstances, to let Jim know how poor the condition of the horse actually was. It was admirable that Jim had made the decision to sell the horses that meant so much to him, and with his health steadily worsening, he did not need anything else to worry about. We lived just around the corner, so I would be checking on the situation regularly.

The boy reluctantly agreed, and I went in the house to say good-bye to Jim. I told him that the baby was all right but had a cold so we would leave him behind for a few days. We said that the boy had graciously agreed to care for him until the cold cleared up. As we were leaving, a gentleman happened to pull in the driveway and express an interest in one of the other babies. He had been admiring her for a while, and when he saw our truck in the driveway, he decided to see if she was available. He was a very nice and knowledgeable gentleman, so we agreed to sell him the Morgan filly. That left us with the neglected Morgan in the barn and Breezy, the Quarter Horse/Arab cross that still stood patiently at the fence.

Breezy came home with us that day, although we didn't know much about her except that she had been used for speed events and that she had not been ridden in quite some time. Our goal was to find her a good home because that was what we had told Jim we would do. We rode her and cared for her through the end of the summer and into the fall. She was an exceptional horse, and I could not help but wonder why Jim's family didn't see that in her and want to spend every moment with her. Eventually, I realized that they were not interested in horses, so they never took the time to see that she was a good horse.

Breezy went to live with a family with a son who would use her for speed events and trail riding. She would be his 4-H project the following year and for many years to come.

We kept a close eye on the sick foal we'd left in Jim's barn, and eventually, he came around. The man who had pulled in the driveway the first day returned to take him home as well. We have since lost track of the man who bought the Morgans, but the last time we spoke to him, they were both doing very well.

Our friends who purchased the Arabian colt still own him today. They never gelded him and found their own diamond in the rough, a very versatile stallion. The other little Arabian filly they purchased was sold to a farm nearby and grew into a beautiful mare.

Before he was completely confined to his bed, Jim used to sit at the window and watch the horses play in the pasture. He was a very knowledgeable horse person. I don't know of anything else that could lift Jim's spirits like horses. Even though he was unable to ride them or care for them personally, his eyes would light up just at their mention. Jim could talk for hours about different horses and their bloodlines. The enthusiasm in his voice taught me of the spiritual therapy horses can provide. He had brought them into his family's lives in an attempt to share something he loved wholeheartedly. Unfortunately, he never considered the fact that his family, although they encouraged him to pursue his interests, didn't appreciate horses the way he did.

Jim's situation inspired me to become involved with the North American Riding for the Handicapped Association (NARHA), a network of therapeutic riding centers across the United States and Canada. They have over 680 centers that promote both the physical and mental rehabilitation of people through the use of horses. The NARHA changed my life by helping me to appreciate horses in a new and more spiritual way. I encourage everyone to get involved with NARHA.

As his physical health deteriorated, Jim was unable to sit at the window and appreciate what he so dearly loved. Instead, he was forced to lie in bed and depend on others to care for his horses until he was finally forced to give them up. My emotions get the best of me when I think of Jim's situation.

Jim passed away later that year, and although I felt very guilty for lying to him about the condition of the horses, he was happy to see them in good homes, and he never had to know of their poor condition. Although he was in no condition to care for his own horses, they still brought joy to a man who had so little else in his life. Sometimes, your interests, whatever they may be, are not shared by those around you, and no matter how much you wish that they were, you must accept this. Enjoy and do what you love; however, do not attempt to force your interests on others. Accept that we are all different in our likes and dislikes, and respect and nurture the people in your life.

Chapter Seventeen
Eve

A Christmas Blessing

*C*hristmas is such a wonderful time of the year. I love those cute Christmas cards from your friends with horses on the front, or scenes of beautiful barns decorated in wreaths and holly, or of a quiet morning ride through the newly fallen snow. My favorite card pictures a fire in the fireplace and a family decorating a freshly cut Christmas tree.

One memorable Christmas, times were tough and there wasn't a lot of money. We were struggling to make ends meet. I was working diligently with my writing, but was without a regular income. Bear had seen an ad in the newspaper about a horse for sale, and we were looking for a quiet horse for a client's daughter. The horse was extremely inexpensive, so we called and made an appointment to go see it.

We arrived at his house and met the owner of the mare. We chatted on the way to the barn, and he mentioned that he was a police officer and was too busy to give the horse any attention, so he wanted to sell her. We asked a lot of questions about the mare, but ironically enough, he couldn't answer even the simplest question, such as how old the horse was or how her ground manners were. It was as if he didn't even own the horse because he knew so little about it. He struggled to open the barn door as though it hadn't been opened in a while. I asked him if the horse was his or whether he was selling the horse for someone else. He assured us that she was his horse, but that he had too many other responsibilities to have a horse.

As we walked in the barn, the first thing I noticed was that the water bucket was bone dry and the stall obviously hadn't been cleaned in quite some time. There was hay in the stall but it was moldy and had also been there for a while. Upon first view of the horse, I became sick to my stomach. Her hooves were disgustingly long. She stood at over fifteen hands and was so skinny that you could literally count every rib. The deep sockets under her hipbones were shallow, as was her face. We estimated that she was at the very least 400 pounds underweight. Bear asked the man when the last time he was even out to the barn and he couldn't remember. Was it Tuesday? Maybe it was Monday. This was now Saturday, so the horse had been locked in the dark barn without food or water for at least four days. I don't know why, but all I could think of was that, because this fellow was a police officer, he should naturally be more responsible. I was obviously wrong.

He informed us that he ran out of hay quite a while ago and had been feeding the horse corn flakes and that she really liked them. By the looks of this horse, she would have eaten dog food had someone offered it to her. He told us the price for the horse which, given our financial situation, was a small fortune. Obviously this wasn't a prospective horse for the client we were looking for, so we now had to decide what the best solution was.

I decided to risk insulting him and pointed out that under the current conditions, the horse would most likely be dead within weeks. Bear explained that we were willing to take the horse, feed her, have her hooves trimmed, and get her back on her feet, but to give the man that amount of money for a horse in such poor condition would be ludicrous.

The mare stood in a corner of her stall with her head hung very low, and we listened to the wind howl through the cracks in the walls. It was extremely cold outside, and the windchill factor was below zero. The man replied by saying that he had to get some payment, because he put six months into feeding and caring for her. It was obvious by the look of the horse that his investment had been a small one. I asked him the horse's name, and he couldn't remember. I looked at Bear who was thinking the same thing that I was: We needed to get this mare out of these conditions or she was going to die. We told the man that we would see how much money we could come up with and that we would call later to make him an offer.

We walked silently to the truck, both of us knowing that Christmas was only a few days away and that we had no money. But we also knew that we had to find a way to save this horse. Neither of us had ever committed a crime, but we actually entertained the idea of going and taking the horse in the middle of the night and placing her in a home where she would be safe. We decided against it, especially considering the owner's profession, and set our minds on finding a way to buy her.

In most areas, we would have had the option of calling a rescue organization or the Humane Society, but the officials in our area knew very little about horses. The rule was that there had to be something on the premises to feed the horse—strict guidelines. One local neglect case involved a pony that the authorities had allowed the owner to keep because the woman showed the Humane Society agent a loaf of bread. The pony died a few days later. If the authorities had considered bread a suitable replacement for a healthy meal, surely corn flakes would have sufficed.

When we got home, we told Jennifer about the mare, and both she and Dusty offered to take back their Christmas presents to save the horse. Bear and I had not purchased gifts for each other in an effort to save money, and here we were trying to buy a horse.

We lay awake most of the night discussing options that ranged from using the payment on the farm, which was already late, or risk getting the utilities shut off. Neither were real options and we both knew it. Our only hope was to ask someone to purchase the horse as an investment. My mom and dad were just getting ready to go to

Florida for the winter, and we hoped they would purchase the mare. We could tell by her conformation that she had once been a good-looking horse and with some food and proper care, we could sell her and make back all the money, if not more.

I called my dad and explained the situation to him, and he said he had some money that he would be willing to invest in the horse. Dad still loved horses at this point, but he had not owned one in quite some time. We agreed that Bear and I would buy the horse for him and work on getting her back in shape over the next few months, and then sell her so my dad could get his money back. I explained to him the possibility of losing the horse because of the condition she was in, and he agreed to take the risk. I called the owner and left a message on his voicemail with the amount we would be willing to offer him for the mare, adding that if he was interested, he should call me back. We would then use the rest of the money to get her vaccinated, wormed, and trimmed. I stayed by the phone all day, and just as I was about to give up, he called and accepted the deal.

I made arrangements for Bear and Jennifer to pick up the horse in the morning. The next day was Christmas Eve, and Bear and Jen got up very early and went to get the horse. Dad came over and watched as Bear unloaded her and turned her out in the front pasture. He put a heavy winter blanket on her to haul her home so that she would be warm, but also because we didn't want my dad to see how sickly she looked until we could prepare him. When we took off the blanket to show my father his new mare, she actually looked worse than she had the day before. Maybe the dark barn had camouflaged the deep shadows on her bony body. Her eyes were sunken and she looked like a skeleton. She went immediately to the water and began to drink it down. We let her have a little and then removed it, because she hadn't had water in a while. We had to be extremely careful with her food as well, because we didn't want to risk colic or founder.

Dad was very quiet as he stood there and watched the mare struggle with the cold. We put her blanket back on but left her out in the corral. She had been locked in that barn for so long and needed to move around a little. We gave Dad a receipt that named him as her owner and thanked him for his help. We agreed that once we got the mare on her feet, we would sell her. He would receive a return on his initial investment, and we would be reimbursed for grain, hay, and anything else she would need.

After seeing how bad the mare actually was, my dad honestly did not think that he would ever see his money again, but he refrained from mentioning it. We said goodbye to him and wished them a safe trip to Florida. They were leaving the following day for Fort Lauderdale, and we didn't know if we would be able to attend the Christmas Eve dinner at their house that night. We just couldn't leave the mare for that length of time.

Early the next morning, I went out to the barn while everyone else was asleep and found my dad standing quietly watching the mare. They were getting ready to pull out but he wanted to take one more look at the horse. We stood there in the early morning light in my barn and talked about the horse, reminiscing about the horse that Dad had owned when I was young. We laughed and talked for almost two hours before he left. It was snowing, and the morning was very quiet.

I was given a very special gift that Christmas morning, quality time with my dad. With six children, it seemed he never had very much quality time to give. Just two days before, all I could do was worry about money and how we would make it through these hard times, but this was a Christmas morning that seemed filled with magic and promise and hope. Bear made coffee and we talked a little more before Dad left, and we promised him that we would keep him informed of how his investment was doing.

We decided to name the mare Eve because it seemed to suit her, and we had brought her home on Christmas Eve. This mare and the efforts to save her became top priority for our family. Everyone pitched in, and to this day, it was one of the best Christmases I can recall. Bear and I wanted nothing more than the opportunity to save this horse, and we received that wonderful gift.

Eve spent the next few weeks getting trimmed, wormed, vaccinated, and fed. She was allowed as much hay as she could eat but we weren't sure if she had seen grain in a while, so we had to slowly reintroduce it to her.

We watched this mare transform from the skinny lifeless creature that we were unsure would even live, to a thriving, beautiful mare. She had energy and stamina and moved with such grace that it was hard to believe she was the same horse. She was willing and proud and pranced with her head held high. She seemed grateful and would call to us from the barn with great enthusiasm. When we introduced her to the other horses, they accepted her into the herd right away. She had her second chance at life.

Dad called often to see how Eve was doing and was pleased with her progress. Spring would be here soon, and they would be returning from Florida. It was time to find Eve a home. We had put a lot of time into her and she was ready. An interested buyer from Michigan wanted a horse that she could teach to jump. Eve was a Thoroughbred and was built for fence work. The prospective buyer came down to our place to ride her, and they clicked immediately. She made us an offer on Eve, and we were very pleased. We accepted it and hauled her to the woman's barn to see where Eve would be living. It was a very nice barn with a pasture that went on forever, and there was a huge pond in the middle of it. It was a far cry from the sad existence Eve had endured before, and we knew she would be happy there.

We called Dad in Florida and told him that he had just tripled his initial investment, and thanked him again for believing in us enough to help us save the horse. Everything had turned out perfectly, and the experience taught us that sometimes, when all other hope is lost, you just have to believe that everything will turn out for the best.

We were extremely blessed that year and received gifts that weren't wrapped in pretty packages with shiny paper and ribbons and bows, but rather gifts of the heart. The wonderful feeling of saving a horse, an early morning visit with my dad that I will never forget, and a horse that brought my entire family closer together. Not a single Christmas goes by that we don't stop and think of Eve and what a blessing she was in our lives when we needed one most.

Chapter Eighteen
The Mexican Pony

Trust

A couple of my friends who are Professional Rodeo Cowboys Association (PRCA) team ropers own a ranch just south of San Antonio in a small town called Junction. One year, they invited Kate, a friend of mine, and me to come down and work on the ranch for a couple of days. We would be rounding up Angora goats and bringing them in for shearing. Aside from a day of riding and rounding up the goats, we would be working with three ranch hands performing their regular duties, such as checking the water supply for their herd and anything else that was considered their daily routine. With great enthusiasm, I got on a plane and headed to Texas. I would be gone only four days because I was scheduled to cover a rodeo in Indianapolis the following weekend. I would need to get back so that I could leave for Indiana and get some interviews for an article I was writing.

From the moment I arrived at the ranch, I immediately felt at ease with my new surroundings. The guys—Kelly, Lee, and Stacy— would be our hosts. Kelly owned the ranch, and Lee and Stacy worked the ranch with him. They spent the first day showing me the finer points of handling a lariat and sharing stories of the different ranches that they had worked for over the years.

That night, we all headed up to the local dance hall for some good music and the opportunity to meet a few more of the local residents. The next day, I was treated to an old-fashioned barbecue in true Texas style. It was a good day. When I left the party to turn in, I couldn't sleep, so I took a walk. I was blessed with the solitude of sitting out on the open range. There was complete darkness with the exception of occasional flashes of lightning from a distant thunderstorm. I was sitting among cattle and horses, and I couldn't see my hand in front of my own face. Every time the lightning flashed, I would get a quick glimpse of the animals that surrounded me. Each time, they came closer, until I could actually feel their breath on the back of my neck. Here I was sitting out on the open range all by myself, surrounded by animals and faced with an approaching thunderstorm, and yet for some reason, I wasn't at all afraid.

That night taught me a lot about trust. I felt totally within my own element. As a writer, I don't remember ever being as inspired as I was enjoying the solitude and overwhelming silence of that night. As much as I would have liked to stay out there forever, I eventually turned in because I knew morning would come all too soon.

When I woke the following morning, I was a little apprehensive but excited about the day that lay ahead. We rounded up the horses that would be used that day and loaded them and the tack in the trailer. We ate breakfast at a quaint little Mexican restaurant where the guys filled us in on exactly what the plan was for rounding up the goats and bringing them to the pens.

Since I had flown, I didn't have the privilege of riding a familiar horse. Not only would I be taking part in an experience that was totally unfamiliar to me but also riding out on a horse that I didn't know at all. It was the opportunity of a lifetime, and, although I was a bit nervous, I wouldn't have missed it for the world.

We finished our breakfast and headed out to where we would saddle up. I wasn't sure which of the horses I would be riding until we arrived. Once there, they gave me a small gelding. He was maybe fourteen hands, which by Ohio standards was actually a pony. They said that he didn't have a name and that he had come from a nearby ranch just a few weeks earlier. He was originally from Mexico and appeared to be extremely laid back.

Kate had no desire to work the range that day, so she rode double with Kelly, and we all headed out. We came to this large hill or small mountain, depending on how you looked at it, that was covered with cactus and trees and goats scattered for as far as I could see. We dropped Kate off at the bottom of the hill, where she would take pictures instead of riding, and proceeded to ride toward our day's work.

The first obstacle we came to was a dry, rock-strewn riverbed. It was extremely deep with an incline almost straight down. In Ohio, where I am from, the landscape does not include large rocks everywhere. I was afraid to take the small horse over the rocks. I hesitated for a moment and looked at Lee. He immediately sensed my hesitation and told me that we would have to cross the riverbed to get to our destination. I agreed and started down the incline. My pony was more than willing, even though it seemed that for every step he took, we would slide about three feet before he would regain his footing enough to take another step. With each step, we were picking up speed due to the fact that we were going straight down the hill as opposed to traversing the hill as you would do if you were skiing. This was my first mistake. The pony tripped on a rock and threw a shoe.

I had heard the guys hollering from behind me, warning me to keep it slow and weave back and forth going down the steep hill, but it was too late. In our part of Ohio, it's flat land, so I had never experienced riding down hills strewn with large rocks and boulders. I felt like the rider from the movie *The Man from Snowy River,* going straight down this hill way too fast. Once we reached the bottom, we proceeded to climb the other side with more caution. I did this in part because the trip down was so rough, but also because my pony was now wearing only three shoes.

There are several very important lessons to be learned out on the open range that you don't necessarily get the opportunity to learn in an Ohio arena. One is the proper way to ride down into a dry riverbed. You would think that the *Snowy River* method would be the quickest and it really is, but it's definitely not the safest.

Once we reached the top of the hill, we saw a herd of approximately 300 goats scattered all over the hillside. The plan was to spread out and work them toward the fence line, where we would drive the herd slowly toward the pens. We would be out for approximately eight hours, and I was on a pony that I knew very little about. Back home, I was riding every day and was showing quite a bit. I was team penning and trail riding, so I really thought I was ready for what lie ahead. I just knew that it would be a while before I would be able to get back to Texas again, so I wanted to spend the day having as much fun as I could. I also wanted to work hard and prove to myself that I could do this.

I'd assumed that working goats would be pretty much the same thing as working cattle, but I couldn't have been more wrong. Goats are smaller, faster, and a lot more difficult to gather and keep in a herd. Lee had neglected to inform me that although blowing the herd (running at them, causing them to scatter) can be a lot of fun in team penning, it isn't recommended with these goats. They are sensitive little creatures that have heart attacks fairly easily. Sometimes, when you rope them, they lose a horn and bleed a lot as well. I was learning all kinds of very useful information.

As we were working the herd down the fence line with Lee carrying a goat who had lost a horn, one of the other goats strayed from our little herd. The pony I was riding had, until now, seemed as though he really didn't have any ambition at all. Maybe it was because he was missing a shoe or because he was silently laughing at me for all of my mistakes, I don't know. Whatever the reason, he didn't seem to want to go any faster than a walk—or, with enough encouragement, a grudging trot. Lee hollered to me to trust the pony, but of course, I was sure that I knew more about riding than the pony did. After all, I needed speed, and this pony hadn't shown me any.

Then the pony realized that we were going after the stray. That little Mexican pony kicked it into high gear and was covering the goats before I could even say go. The first place the goat headed for was cover. He ducked under a tree that resembled a crab apple tree. It had low hanging, sharp branches that came to about my chest. The pony cleared the tree with no problem. He didn't care that I didn't clear it, he only wanted the stray. I cued him to cut left around the tree and he went right instead. The branch from the tree grabbed hold of the back of my shirt and tore it straight across the shoulder. I managed to stay on but almost lost my shirt in the process. I could hear Lee laughing under his breath as he rode over to see whether I was all right. He was still carrying the goat with the broken horn, and it had now bled all over the front of his shirt and down the side of his gray horse. We were quite a pair. I was sure that had I not been there, he would have had a much more productive day, but at least I was entertaining.

We met up with Kelly just after I tore my shirt. There was a baby goat that had been left behind by his mother, so I took it upon myself to scoop him up and stick him down the front of what was left of my shirt and carry him for the rest of the day. These are dirty little animals with fleas and the worst smell you can imagine, but I just couldn't leave him behind.

The guys laughed at me riding the rest of the afternoon with a screaming goat tucked down my shirt. As soon as I got the chance, I rode down the hill and left the baby with Kate, who was capturing it all with her camera. We finished taking the herd down to the pens and called it a day. The baby goat was left with the rest of the herd, and I was ready to go back to the ranch for a shower. Kelly rode back to get Kate, and we loaded the horses and headed out to check water.

Since it was early spring and had been such a dry winter, the water supply was a deep well with a pump powered by a windmill. It took us about another twenty minutes to check the series of water throughout the ranch and although I smelled like goat, I had a torn shirt, and every muscle in my body ached beyond belief, it had been a great day. We met the others at the house and by the time we got back to the barn to turn the horses out and put the tack away, I was so tired that I skipped dinner and actually slept with my boots on.

Trust the horse you ride, and trust the people in your life. Remember the dance—it's about making them your partner and respecting them when it comes to their own element. I was someone the pony had just met and I'm sure, given enough time to work with him, that respect would have been returned. Even though I did feel that the pony should have been more responsive to my cues, I underestimated his ability to do his job. The Mexican pony had obviously done this work before and knew exactly what needed to be done without my interference.

I still have the shirt I wore that day as a constant reminder to myself to be ready for anything, to trust the person or animal who is trying to teach me something new, and to never presume to know more than he or she does. Like some people, horses are incredibly smart, and if there is one thing that remains consistent, it's that they will always surprise you. Learn to love the dance, and the result will be pure magic.

Chapter Nineteen
Dakota's Pride

High Expectations

*D*akota's Pride (Pride, for short) was a pretty little Paint gelding we had met after a woman, Sue, lost her sister in a tragic car accident. The two women had been extremely close, and Sue decided that it hurt far too much to look at the horse because Dakota had been her sister's horse. To Sue, Pride was a constant reminder of a lifetime of good memories shared and a beautiful friendship lost.

Sue called us and explained her situation. It was obvious that she was deeply upset about giving up one more part of her sister by selling Pride, but the unbearable grief she felt each time she looked at the horse was more than she could bear.

I could certainly relate to the fact that we sometimes associate people we lose with the horses they loved. There are times when I can't remember a person I've met, no matter how that person is described to me, but mention the horse that the person rides, and I remember that person immediately.

My heart went out to Sue as I listened to her painfully explain the events that had transpired in her life over the previous year. I have three sisters, and, although we don't always get along, I still love them. The thought of losing any one of them brings tears to my eyes.

I had met Sue and her sister briefly on a trail ride a year before, and in our conversation, I had admired Pride. He had not been started under saddle, as he was still quite young then. They had taken him just to get him used to the trailer and to being in the park. We had exchanged phone numbers on the trail, and I hadn't heard from them again until this day.

Sue explained that in the months that followed her sister's death, she had struggled with the idea of selling the horse. She went on to say that she had thought long and hard about this decision, and after running across my phone number and remembering how much I liked Pride, she decided that if I wanted to buy the horse, she would sell him to me. She thought that selling him would be the best thing for her and the horse.

During the several months that followed her sister's accident, Sue had leased Pride to a family that had decided he was no longer the cute little baby they wanted, but rather a grown horse with a mind of his own. They eventually lost interest in him. Other than taking care of his basic needs, he was left turned out with a herd of other horses, totally within his natural element. She explained that she had gone back to the people's barn after she had made the decision and now realized that working with Pride would be like starting all over with him from day one. Sue was honest about the fact that roaming free with other horses on thirty acres with no interaction with people had changed Pride substantially.

We discussed arrangements for getting him to my barn, and I agreed to mail a check to her. She would call the barn where he was boarded and let them know we were coming.

I spent the evening thinking about how sad she had sounded on the phone, and I found it strange that Sue had even remembered me at all from such a brief encounter on the trails. What was more odd was that this call came from out of the blue from someone I honestly couldn't remember meeting. Sue had given me an extremely detailed account of the day and nothing about the story sounded familiar. Despite the fact that I couldn't remember Sue or her sister, in my mind's eye, I could see the horse. Something—call it instinct—told me that I was supposed to go get this horse and bring him home.

I clearly remember the evening Bear went to get Pride. It was snowing, the biggest flakes I had ever seen. It was soft, fluffy snow, there was absolutely no breeze, and the temperature was very mild. The reason I remember it so clearly is because there was lightning that lit up the sky. In my life, I have witnessed lightning during a heavy snowfall only twice. The first time was when I was in labor with my second daughter, Jennifer, and was on my way to the hospital. It was a magical night.

On the night that Pride entered our lives, I was in my barn, cleaning stalls and making room for the hay that Bear was bringing home. As I watched him pull up to the barn, I had an overwhelming feeling of deja vu. It was magical, comforting, and peaceful, and the feeling intensified the eeriness of the weather.

Bear pulled around to the barn with our twenty-foot trailer that had replaced the little red two-horse trailer we had once owned. It was a gooseneck, and the back was filled with hay. He had picked up Pride first, so he was in the front section of the trailer munching on whatever hay he could reach during the ride home.

We unloaded the hay as Pride stood there and watched us, very calmly looking around as the other horses called to him. Bear walked him out of the trailer, and I was awestruck at his beauty. He was not quite 3 years old, and all legs. He had not yet filled out into his adult physique.

Pride was afraid of nothing. Because he'd had very little contact with people, he responded to things by looking to the other horses for their reaction. Ironically, when we unloaded him from the trailer, he immediately looked to us to see whether he should be afraid of something. We walked him to the barn with no problem at all. Even as the dogs ran up barking, although curious and a little startled at first, Pride was not afraid because he saw that we didn't react to them. He turned to look at them, stepping on my feet, but merely wanting to get a good look. His initial response to new situations was one of curiosity instead of apprehension. He was one of the calmest horses I had ever met.

Pride had spent most of his life without being exposed to new things. He had been turned out on open land with other horses so he was never taught about all that was possible. I grew up, as so many other children had, with limited resources and, therefore, limited exposure to what is possible. I was exposed to horses, and my immediate love for them changed my life forever. I often wonder what my life would be like had my parents not nurtured that love; if all I had been exposed to was living in the inner city and moving from place to place. I would most likely still be living in the city, moving my children to a new house or apartment once or twice a year. We can only achieve what we know in our lives, but if we have the opportunity to expand our horizons, or the horizons of those around us, the possibilities are endless. My father envisioned a better life for us outside the city. It was a life that I would not have dreamed for myself, because I didn't know how wonderful it could be. It is our responsibility to nurture the people around us, especially children. It is our responsibility to show children all that is possible and to encourage them to look beyond what they know.

As with people, everything we do with our horses will shape their personality in some way. We needed to expose Pride to everything, just as we had done with Teddy. We would need to do it calmly and quietly so that he would not fear new things. A horse who has not experienced a lot of interaction with people is like a clean slate. He has no preconceived ideas about so many things. We find it much easier to start fresh with horses than to be responsible for undoing any bad habits that were imprinted on them in the past.

Pride was extremely intelligent and very eager to learn. We started him under saddle, and, amazingly enough, he learned quickly just as with everything else we taught him. Sometimes a quiet, easygoing horse can teach you every bit as much as one that continually challenges you. We were spending a lot of time with

Pride and thoroughly enjoying every minute. At the time, we had had a long run of starting horses that were a constant challenge, and it was a welcome relief to simply enjoy a good-minded, easygoing horse.

One day, a friend of ours stopped by and showed interest in riding Pride. Matt had ridden bulls and broncs. We tease him that his butt is made of Velcro, because in all the years we've known him, he has never come off a horse. Horses have tried really hard to get him off, but he always manages to stay on. We were happy to have Matt expose Pride to some new things and encouraged him to give Pride a try. Matt preferred riding bareback, so one day while Bear was at work, we put a bridle on Pride, and Matt crawled up on his back. We had finished the basics on Pride, but we had actually only been riding him for a few weeks.

Bear and I were still getting Pride comfortable with a new rider and had no intention of asking Pride to do very much at all. Although we had been riding him, it was mostly round pen basics, so this was the first time that he had been in a larger area without any horses in sight. Because of their herd instincts, many horses are very sensitive to riding alone in an open arena at first. One way to get them past this fear is to ride another horse and *pony,* or lead, the young horse close by. The other way, of course, is just to test the waters.

Matt swung up on Pride's back and just sat there for a moment. Pride planted all four feet and tipped his ears back, which told us that Matt had his full attention. They weren't laid back in an aggressive way, but rather just enough to listen to what was going on behind him. Matt gently squeezed with his legs, and Pride took a couple of steps forward and stopped again. He didn't put up a fight at all. Each horse can be taken to different levels and at different speeds. Pride trusted us and could therefore be asked to do more than most other horses. Matt asked him to trot, and then to canter; Matt used his legs to signal to Pride which way he wanted him to turn, and Pride complied.

Eventually Matt was asking Pride to canter on the rail next to the jumps that were out in the arena, and Matt gave him free rein to allow him to go around the jumps at first. We wanted to keep the mood light and not ask too much of him. Pride moved up to the jump instead, and cleared it with no problem. Had the jumps not been there, he would not have been exposed to the opportunity, and we would not have known that he had a natural ability for jumping. Matt and I played with him for about an hour, taking turns riding him and allowing him to take a jump now and then. Pride loved it. Although he seemed to be begging to learn more, we didn't want to push him along too quickly.

Like Matt, I have always preferred to ride bareback and usually never rode with a saddle unless I was out on a long trail ride or in the show ring. Pride was so comfortable to ride bareback. He almost never spooked, which was good in the sense that he wouldn't carry on over frivolous things; however, it was not so good in the sense that he gave absolutely no warning when something did frighten him. Pride was not a very emotional horse, which made him difficult to read at times. There are so many people that we think we know, only to find out at some point that they are not the people that we thought they were because they are difficult to read. Take your time with these people and listen well.

After a few months of working with Pride, teaching him new things, and learning more life lessons from him, we tried to contact Sue to let her know how well he was doing and ask her if she wanted to come over for a visit. Try as I might, I still could not remember having ever met her or her sister. I tried the number she had left, and a woman answered, but it wasn't Sue. I verified the number and asked if she had recently changed her number. She told me that she had never heard of Sue, and that she had had the same number for several years. That weekend, we drove by the farm where Pride had lived, and there was a "FOR SALE" sign in the front yard. There were no horses in the pasture, no cars in the drive, and no curtains in the windows of the house. The check that I gave her for Pride never cleared, which meant she never cashed it. I could have called the real estate agent and inquired further but I am a firm believer in following your instinct, and my instinct told me to let it go. Sometimes, unexplainable events occur in our lives that seem nothing short of divine intervention. Embrace them and be grateful for them and do not question where they came from. Just thank God that they did come and learn from the experience.

It is my experience that horses will do whatever is expected of them, within reason. The same holds true for people. Being clear on what is expected, knowing limitations, and encouraging them to set their goals and stay on a constant path toward achieving their goals is what's important. If a child is born with limited expectations and opportunities, how will that child grow to be an adult who believes that anything is possible? Encouragement! Nurturing children by encouraging them and showing them what is possible creates an adult who sees and believes and achieves anything. I strongly believe that Pride was meant to teach us about setting higher expectations for ourselves in an effort to grow as individuals through new experiences; to show us what is possible beyond what we know within our own lives. He was meant to teach me to challenge myself, to try new things and to trust in my abilities.

Shortly after Pride left us, I had a very exciting opportunity offered to me, and I took it. I would normally have had reservations, because it was not something I had ever been exposed to. My fear would have taken over, and I would have passed on it. But not this time. So one cold, snowy day, I strapped a harness with a parasail to my back and ran behind a pickup truck in an open field until the wind caught my sail and lifted me 150 feet in the air. It was the most exciting feeling, flying above the tree line in the cold brisk air, but what excited me the most, and still does when I think about it, was that I had the courage to do it at all!

I will always remember the night we brought Pride home, and over the years, I have come to realize how much his personality was like that quiet night with the lightning off in the distance. Pride was one of a kind, just like all of the horses that we meet and love. Horses can teach us volumes about ourselves and the people in our lives. Once you take the time to really get to know them, the possibilities are endless.

Chapter Twenty
The Sorrel Mare

Disappointment

*O*f all the horses we've known, this horse probably taught us more about the darker side of people than any other. We dearly loved her, but for the sake of this story, I will refer to her only as the sorrel mare. She taught us about disappointment and finding your true strength of character when it comes time for forgiveness. Before Charlie died, Jen had considered using her as her 4-H project. In our county, members must have their horse in their possession by June 1, because our fair is in September, and we encourage the kids to work with their own horses. This not only makes the competitive part of 4-H more equal, in the sense that the kids are working with their own horses, but it gives them a greater feeling of accomplishment as well. So Jen, like so many of the kids, was looking for a horse to use for her project.

Just after we lost Charlie and her foals, a friend of mine, Leslie, called with a very generous offer. I had known Leslie since we were young kids and used to ride with her at Mr. Metcalf's barn. We had lost touch over the years, but became friends again when our daughters became active in showing horses. Leslie's daughter Melanie was older than Jen and had just joined the Navy. She was due to leave in a few months. Leslie lived with her mom and dad and her two sons, Melanie's younger brothers. The sorrel mare belonged to Melanie, but no one had seriously ridden her in a few years.

Leslie and her parents had eight horses at their barn, which was basically more like a garage with stalls. They had a nice turnout area, but the stalls were extremely small, with barely enough room to move around. Leslie's mom didn't ride at all, but she liked the horses a lot, so she never parted with any of them. She had cancer and hardly ever got out to the barn, which left Leslie and her dad to care for the horses.

When Leslie found out that we had lost Charlie, she called out of the blue and offered us the sorrel mare. She had asked several times about breeding a mare to Beau, but never seriously enough to sign a contract. She explained that between Melanie leaving for the Navy and she and her dad not having the time to care for all of their horses, Leslie needed to find homes for at least a couple of them. I declined at first, because we knew how large the bill had been for all of the veterinary care Charlie had received in our attempt to save her. We just weren't in a position to spend a lot of money on buying and caring for this mare. Leslie offered us the horse for free, with no conditions at all. I knew that Jen had remembered the mare from her days of showing and had seen how difficult she could be. Now the mare had been left to stand for a long time, and her attitude had probably worsened. I explained this to Leslie and thanked her for the generous offer, but declined.

Bear and I talked to Jen and decided that we still had time to find her another horse before the June 1 deadline. About three days later, Leslie called again to tell us she was in the hospital with pneumonia. Her dad was sick as well. She asked us if we would go feed the horses and clean their stalls, because they had been locked up in the barn for three days. She was completely out of hay, and it was the middle of winter, so there was very little hay available to buy. Bear and I agreed to take her horses some hay and stack it in their barn, turn out their horses, and feed and water them all.

When we arrived, the horses had no water and were obviously upset that they had not been fed or turned out to exercise. The sorrel mare had kicked down the wall of her stall between herself and a small crippled Arab mare who was next to her. The wall, which had just been scrap pieces of plywood held together with nails, now had exposed nails showing. The mare was pinning her ears and kicking at the little crippled mare. She tried to bite us when we went near her. It was already getting dark, so we handed the Arab to Leslie's son who had gone out to the barn with us. He refused to take either of the horses because he was afraid of them. I turned one of them out in a small paddock and held the other while Bear patched the stall enough that it would hold until Leslie or her dad could fix it properly. We cleaned the stalls and fed and watered the horses. We stacked twenty bales of hay in the shed, which was enough to hold them over for a while. We went home feeling as though we should have taken Leslie up on her offer just to get the sorrel mare out of there and make a little more room for the other horses, but decided against it.

The next day, we got a call from Leslie's mom, who told us that she would really like us to have the sorrel mare. In exchange, she had always wanted a foal out of our stallion so we could breed her other mare, a cute little Palomino, as a trade for the horse. We told her that we would think about it and thanked her for the offer. Jen had decided at this point that the sorrel mare needed a lot of work and might be too much for her to handle, so even if we did make the trade, she was not sure she had an interest in showing her.

The last thing Leslie and her family really needed was a foal to care for. They didn't have a stall large enough to house a foaling mare, and we knew it. They had once bred the small Arab mare there and had a lot of problems.

That night, Leslie called from the hospital and told us that the sorrel mare had kicked down the wall again, and the horses had yet to be turned out after about a week. We knew they had not gotten water, since we had to carry buckets from the house to water them the last time, and no one was up to that because they were still too sick. She begged us to go and get the mare and bring her to our barn; we could just have her. She would give us a receipt for the mare when she got out of the hospital if we went and got her.

Bear and a friend of ours went over to the barn, and found that the situation had worsened. Now the mare had a cut on her leg from the exposed nails and was clearly sore from kicking through her stall. Bear and our friend fed and watered the horses and cleared the boards from the stall so the little Arab mare would have room to move. Then they loaded the sorrel mare into the trailer for the ride to our barn. She kicked the trailer all the way home and then proceeded to try and tear down our barn once we got her there. We turned her out the first thing in the morning, and she was immediately calm. She still didn't want anyone near her, but we worked on that a little at a time. Every time we put her back in a stall, she started in again kicking the walls, trying to go over the top of the wall to bite at the horse next to her, and weaving back and forth.

At one time, years ago, when this horse was with a proper handler on a full-time basis, I had shown her in a pleasure class, and she rode beautifully. I knew this horse was capable of so much more, but I also knew that she had been left to stand for a long time and had not been treated with the best of care. Leslie and her family were going through tough times, and they just couldn't give the mare the attention she needed. We called them once Leslie was out of the hospital and attempted to make arrangements to bring the mare back. They insisted that they didn't want her and that she was ours now. We were all still extremely tired after our ordeal with losing Charlie and dealing with the emotional aspect of it as well. Now, here we were, going out to the barn to check on this horse, turning her out every few hours so she would get used to the confinement again, and repairing the damage to our barn on a daily basis. Although we greatly appreciated Leslie's generosity in offering us the mare, we were just drained.

Our farrier, who was also a very good friend of ours at the time, came to trim the mare's hooves. We wormed her and gave her a vaccination for the spring. The weather was getting nicer and the nights were warmer, so we followed the farrier's suggestion to turn her out in the small paddock behind the barn. We put another horse in the paddock next to her so she would not be alone and brought her in only when the weather turned bad. She was putting on weight, and her attitude was improving. I called Leslie about the papers on her, and she told me that they had lost them. She told me she would call the American Quarter Horse Association (AQHA) and get another set.

Spring was fast approaching, and Leslie and her mom were encouraging us on a regular basis to go ahead and breed the sorrel mare to Beau. They felt that we would get a nice foal out of her for ourselves. There was no more talk about breeding the little Palomino mare. We had mixed feelings about breeding the sorrel mare, after all we had been through, and we assumed that with everything that was going on, Leslie and her family had realized that it wasn't such a good idea for them to have a foaling mare at their barn. However, they were very encouraging about getting on with our lives and getting the sorrel mare bred, so we had the vet come out and give her a thorough exam to make sure that everything was all right and that we could indeed breed her. The vet said she was ready, so we proceeded. It was getting close to the time that Jen would have to make a decision about her project for 4-H. Although we had been working with the sorrel mare quite a bit and she was coming around, Jen was still leaning toward either using another horse or just passing on the year and taking a break from 4-H.

Leslie's mom called Jen and asked her if she would take the sorrel mare as her project, saying how happy it would make her to come and watch Jen show her at the fair. After much consideration, Jen agreed, and we signed her up with the mare. At this point, I needed the papers on the horse for Jen's 4-H file, so I asked Leslie for them again. She said that she had found a copy of the papers and we could use those until she got the originals from AQHA. She would just sign a free lease agreement until she could get her transferred into Jen's name. A free lease is a written agreement, stipulating that Jen would have permission to use the horse as her project.

Jen and I worked with the mare every day to get her ready for the 4-H fair. She was now easier to handle on the ground, but when we took her to work sessions she would buck and carry on, and Jen would come off and get back on. She had a real fight on her hands. A couple of times, the mare even lay down with Jen on her back. Jen scrambled out of the way in time, but it could have been a disaster.

Bear and I tried to talk Jen out of using the horse, but she was determined to ride her, so we spent every free moment working with her. We called Leslie and her mom every day with updates on the mare's progress and to thank them again for giving her to us. We invited them to shows where Jen was showing her, and they didn't show up. The only thing they wanted to know was whether or not the mare had definitely been bred. We found that strange, because it would be our foal, not theirs. Each time they called, we would ask if they had gotten the registration papers to sign her over to us legally. They had not.

We put so much time into this mare, that I had very little time to ride any of the other horses. One day, I had gotten her out to work with her. It was a Friday, and we had a show the next morning in Findlay, Ohio, with Beau. I only had a short time to work with the mare, because I had to pack the trailer and get ready. I had her on the lead line and was walking her back to the barn after I had ridden her. She was dancing around and acting like she had no manners at all. Beau was pacing the fence line, and he called to her. She spun toward me to see Beau on the other side of me, and, as she did, she smacked me in the side of my temple with her head. I immediately felt the pain shoot through my head and saw white spots for a few moments. I waited until it passed, and then got her back under control and put her away. By the time I finished up in the barn and got in the house, I was really tired and had a headache. I called Bear and told him that I was going to lie down for a while. He said we would finish packing for the show when he got home from work and he would help me get Beau bathed and clipped.

I slept for a few hours and when I woke, I felt as though I was still tired. I had a lot to do, so I got up and went back to packing. The light bothered both my eyes for a while, but as the day wore on, I really didn't feel all that bad. I was still tired, so I went to bed early, and when it was time to leave the next morning, it was still dark outside. I took some aspirin for my headache and we went to the show. After my first class, I noticed that the light was bothering my eyes a lot more, especially my right eye, which was the side the mare had hit with her head. The first class was a color class, so it was outside in the sun. Everything seemed brighter, and the sun hurt my eyes. I took two more aspirin and went in the indoor arena for Bear's halter class, where it seemed darker than usual. Bear told me to go home and rest; if it was still bothering me on Monday, I would go to the doctor and have it checked. Sunday was fine; although the light still bothered my eyes a bit and my temple was sore to the touch, it wasn't bad enough to go to the hospital.

Monday morning, I slept in until Bear and Jen had already left. When I opened my eyes, everything looked fuzzy, so I rubbed them but things didn't clear. I got up and went into the bathroom and turned on the light. I could see all right out of my left eye, but the right eye was like looking through a hazy tube. I could see very little off to the right side and in front of me, it was blurry. It felt scratched or swollen, as though I had something in my eye. I called the doctor and he told me to come in. He examined me and sent me to an eye specialist, who dilated my eyes and ran a series of tests. He explained that I had lost the peripheral vision in my right eye and that it might come back or it might not. It was then determined that the blood vessels that led to my optic nerve were extensively damaged. We would have to see how it was once the swelling behind my eye went down. He explained that it could take as long as six months and that my vision may return to normal, but there were no guarantees. If it did not return after the swelling went down, he could perform surgery in an attempt to repair any damage, but there was a 50 percent chance that the surgery could cause me to lose my vision in that eye completely. At this point, we would just have to wait and see what happened.

Getting used to the partial loss of vision was difficult. We would go in stores, and I would walk into things on my right. I would misjudge doorways at first and walk into walls or trip over the dog if he didn't move. I would sit in the bathtub at night and count the day's bruises, and there were some days I would just cry out of fear and frustration. My vision wasn't getting any better; if anything, it was slowly getting worse. Although it had been my choice to bring the mare to our barn and work with her, I was incredibly angry at the situation. I thought about Dewey, my family's first experience with a horse, and how he had learned to adjust to his blindness and to his surroundings. Again, I would learn a very important lesson from a horse in trying to adjust to my condition.

Eventually, I got my center of balance adjusted and could do all the things that I had always done. I just had to be more careful when doing them. But gradually, the sight in that eye worsened and everything got darker. The condition never did resolve itself, and we opted against surgery. Today, my eyes get tired easily, and I have to know when to walk away from the computer or just close my eyes, even if only for ten minutes. Most people don't even notice, and we just don't tell them. There are actually some days that I don't even think about it.

Leading up to our fair, Jen was winning at shows with the sorrel mare and getting better and better. Soon it was time to have the mare ultrasounded to see whether she was bred. We were going to give up and wait until the next year, but in May, Leslie's mom called and said that part of the reason they gave her to us was because they wanted to see us get a baby out of her. This was the year after Charlie died, and the foal would be our new beginning. We set up the ultrasound for the following Monday. We told Leslie that the mare had not come back into season so we were pretty sure that she was bred. We insisted on the ultrasound to be sure that everything was all right. This was Thursday. On Friday morning, I received a call from Leslie telling me that her mom was on her way over, and she wanted the mare back. I was shocked beyond belief.

Leslie said that the farrier had been at their house the night before and told her mom that the mare was standing in mud up to her knees; she was thin and forced to stay out in the weather all the time. I just assumed that it was a misunderstanding and she would get there and see for herself that the mare actually looked better than she had when we got her; the paddock she was in was sand and had runoff drains so it was dry. Not to mention the fact that putting her outside where she would be happier on good days had been the farrier's idea! She was being put in the stall for short periods of time but was kicking the walls, so we would put her out often, but never in bad weather. The barn was clean and dry, and basically the horse could not have been cared for any better.

The last thing Leslie asked me was whether or not we had the ultrasound done yet. That sent up red flags, and I knew that there was more to this than what the farrier had apparently said. Now the farrier was a friendly guy, and Bear and I had always considered him a friend, but we also knew that he was notorious for starting trouble from barn to barn and had actually been banned from a few for this very reason. He was a good farrier, and for him to completely fabricate these allegations when he had a wonderful reputation for caring for our animals was unbelievable. Since it had been his idea to keep her out more often, none of this made any sense at all.

I called him before Leslie arrived, and he was as surprised as I was. He said that they had asked him the night before if he knew whether or not she was bred for sure. He told them he didn't know but suspected that she was. They asked him how she was, and he told them that he had suggested we keep her outside since she was tearing down the barn, and we were doing that. He added that the mare looked great.

Leslie's mom and dad arrived with a truck and trailer, and she immediately began to scream that she was there for the horse. She was using foul language, and her husband just ducked his head in embarrassment. I showed her the horse and the paddock and explained that it was all a misunderstanding, and she proceeded to tell me that she didn't care. She missed the horse and had changed her mind. Jen was out there and was crying, explaining how we had put five months into that horse and if she took her now, Jen could not show her at the fair. She showed Leslie's mom the ribbons she had won on her so far that summer. At this point, Jen was working and showing this mare and caring for her. Not once had any of them even been to the barn in five months nor had they gone to see her show, as they had promised.

Jen was crushed beyond belief, and I was just getting angrier by the minute. I felt as though we had been set up. I told them that until I had the ultrasound done on the horse to see whether or not she was bred, they could not take the horse. I called Bear at work and told him what had happened. We checked with the AQHA because the copy of the papers she had given us were not even in her name. They told us that, at the time Leslie had told me she was ordering another set of papers because she had lost them, they were actually getting the horse registered in their name. Now, if she had true intentions of giving Jen the horse, I wondered if it would not have been just as easy to transfer them into Jen's name instead. Here we had put five months into the care and training of this horse, and we had bred her to Beau, all the while being promised that they would straighten out the papers. I had lost my sight in my right eye as a result of this mess. All in all, it had cost us dearly, and now they just wanted to change their minds and take her back. If they did this and the mare was confirmed bred, they would own the foal that was meant to be ours.

I called the vet who was due to come out and do the ultrasound Monday to see whether she would come out Saturday instead. She told me that Leslie and her mom had been calling her office, wanting to know if the mare was truly bred. She told them that we were her clients and that she would not release any information, and they threatened her. She was angry, we were angry, and Jen was in tears at this point. The vet agreed to come out that afternoon to do the ultrasound. Leslie called, as did her mom, several times insisting that we not do the ultrasound at all, but rather give the horse back. They would have the ultrasound done once she was back in their barn. They had even threatened to sue the vet if she performed the ultrasound, as it would be proof that she was bred. They wanted to take the mare home and have the ultrasound done there so the mare would be in their possession when she was confirmed bred. We were all pretty sure that she was pregnant, but an ultrasound would prove conclusively that there was an impending foal. We could have given the mare a shot to cause her to end the pregnancy, but after what we had been through with Charlie and the foals, we just couldn't do it.

I had told her that if the horse was not bred, we would just cut our losses and send her back to them, but it was obvious that we had been set up so that they could get a free foal. If she were bred, we would keep her until she foaled and then send her back. That's when they admitted that they'd wanted the foal from the beginning.

The ironic part is that Leslie was my friend, or so I'd thought, and Bear and I would have given her family a free breeding if they had asked. Although they had asked to breed the Palomino mare to Beau at one point, they later realized that their barn was not set up to house a mare and foal. As it was, they had destroyed a friendship with greed. They wanted the free training, free board for five months, and the baby as well, and there was absolutely nothing we could do about it because the horse's registration papers were still in their name.

We did the ultrasound, and it showed what we had suspected all along: The mare was bred. They took us to court to get the horse back, and we fought it to enable Jen to finish the season with the mare and take her to fair. The judge basically said that the horse was no different than a car in the eyes of the law. Whoever had registration papers in their name legally owned the horse—and that person was Melanie, the daughter in the Navy. The only compensation we received was $250 for the breeders' certificate once the foal was born and $250 for the foal. Beau's foals were worth at least ten times that. The rest of the money and time we had put into her was lost to us. The agreement did stipulate that Jen could keep the horse until the 4-H fair was over, because we still had the lease agreement that we were using until the registration papers were transferred.

We spent the rest of the summer dealing with constant harassment and threats from these people. When the fair finally came, they actually tore down Jen's stall decorations and ruined her time there. She was so disappointed; she had worked so hard for this day, and their presence ruined everything. Melanie came back from the Navy for the week of the fair and signed the papers that allowed her mother and grandmother to take the horse from us. The judge could not do anything except go by the person who legally owned the horse, whose name was on the registration papers.

It has been said that success is the best revenge, and Jen got her success that day as these people sat in the stands and watched. Jen won Grand Champion Horsemanship with the mare. We made arrangements for Leslie and her family to pick up the horse from the fairgrounds on the last day of the fair. We sent Jen home the night before so she wouldn't have to be there to see her go. To make matters worse, they never showed up. After waiting several hours, we hauled the mare home, and then had to explain to Jen that she still couldn't keep her. We called their attorney and told him that they could meet us at the house at 5:00 the next day and not before, because Jen would be home by herself until then. They parked in the road with the trailer in tow at 3:30 and proceeded to blow the horn until 5:00 when we arrived.

In early May of the following year, the sorrel mare gave birth to a Palomino stud colt. We've driven by their pasture to see him every now and then, and have seen the horses turned out only a few times. We did watch them show the colt at one show a few years later, and he placed last in that class. He was thin and didn't appear to be clipped and bathed properly for the show, and it seemed that the judge dismissed the horse because of it. We never saw the horse at any other shows after that.

Several months later, we ran into Leslie's father, who admitted that his wife and daughter had schemed to get the free training and free foal from the beginning. He apologized, but there was nothing we could do. It was too little, too late.

I can't tell you how I regret the trust that I gave so freely to these people and how much it hurts to relive it through telling this story, but if it saves even one person from making the same mistake, it was well worth it. The best lesson to be learned from all of this is to get everything in writing, no matter what the situation or the people involved. We took their word and their generosity at face value when we should have questioned their motives. Jen was disappointed because she had grown to love that mare. We were disappointed because the foal was to be our new beginning, and now he belonged to someone else.

Disappointment and resentment seem to go hand in hand in some situations, but resentment doesn't resolve anything. Forgive everyone for everything, or the resentment you feel will continue to haunt you for the rest of your life. Forgiveness is a gift that you give to yourself. Hatred and resentment are like a cancer that will destroy you eventually.

Although we want nothing to do with them, we wish Leslie and her family well, and we truly hope that the colt that was born as a result of this was eventually placed with very good people who love him.

Chapter Twenty-One

Sparky

The Miracle of Birth

*W*e have had the privilege of seeing many babies born at our barn. We have witnessed the miracle of birth. We have felt the hand of God touch each one of them as they take their first breath and guide them as they take their first steps. Some have gone on to live a good many years, while others have never seen the light of day. From the first foal to the last, we have known that their fate is out of our hands, and, try as we may, we can't control it beyond giving them the best life possible. That is the rule; however, there is an exception to every rule, and Sparky taught me that.

Cher is my favorite mare here at the barn. She is one of two mares that Bear went all the way to Texas to pick up for me because they were perfect for the foals we hoped to produce. He left for Texas on New Year's Eve and my oldest daughter, Dusty, went in labor shortly thereafter. Jennifer, my younger daughter, and I called the doctor and gave him her condition, and he said that it was false labor. But Dusty was in excruciating pain—when Jen asked her "on a scale from one to ten, what's the level of your pain?" Dusty cried "TWELVE!"—so after several hours, we decided to take her to the hospital anyway.

It's a thirty-mile drive from our house in the country to the hospital, and every painstaking mile seemed like an eternity. It was snowing hard, it was dark, and Dusty was screaming the entire way. At one point, she knelt down on the seat next to me facing the rear of the car and announced that she felt she had to push. I strongly encouraged her not to and drove faster.

When we arrived at the hospital, we were met by a team in the emergency room and taken to labor and delivery. A younger woman came in to check her and stated that she would be right back. After a few minutes, I went into the hallway to find this woman, as the contractions were less than one minute apart. She was nowhere to be seen, so I grabbed another woman, an intern, and asked her whether she could check Dusty's progress. After a quick examination, she picked up the phone next the bed and dialed a number. Her exact words to the person at the other end were, "Get everyone in here immediately, this woman is giving birth NOW!"

She hung up the phone and instructed me to get several items from the drawers near the bed. Giving birth is actually less stressful than aiding in the delivery of another woman giving birth, especially if that woman is your daughter. I did as the intern said, and exactly six minutes after we had entered the room, my first grandson, Garrett, was born. I held him in my arms while the intern clamped and cut the umbilical cord. As a flurry of medical personnel entered the room, it was obvious that the baby was not breathing. They took him from my arms and whisked him to a table on the other side of the room. A neonatal team worked on him, as I held my breath and attempted to keep my daughter calm. At one point, the intern looked over at me and shook her head. It literally took my breath away, as I knew that things did not look good at all. I prayed harder than I have ever prayed in my life, and when Garrett cried for the first time, I knew that my prayers had been answered.

Once things calmed down, I called Bear in Texas to tell him that he was a grandfather. Two days later, he returned home with Cher and her sister Robin, our two new horses. Ironically enough, each of them had a big letter "G" brand on their hips for the name of the ranch from which they had come. To me, it was more than coincidence that they bore a brand with the first letter of my first grandchild's name. In conversations that followed, Dusty would mention that she really didn't understand why I was so upset by the traumatic experience of his birth and the fear of something happening to him; a statement that can easily be made by someone who was sedated in the moments following his birth.

Every year, Cher gave me a nice baby, and she usually delivered without any human intervention whatsoever; try as I may, I never did witness any of her babies actually being born. She would trick me. Either she would give birth a week early or a week late, or she would give birth in the middle of the night when I just closed my eyes for a few hours while watching the monitor in the bedroom. We used to have barn parties and stay up all night for several nights in a row waiting for the mares to foal, but as we got older and smarter, we put up surveillance cameras in the barn so we could watch them on the monitor from the comfort of our own bed.

One summer afternoon, Dusty, who had never had an interest in horses, was over with Garrett for a visit. Garrett was about 3 years old at the time. We were doing yard work and trying desperately to keep an eye on him. It was hot, so we had both the mares, who were due to foal, in the cool of the barn with the fan running. We would go check on them periodically, and both were standing comfortably in their stalls. On one such check, Dusty hollered to me to come quickly; one of the mares, Cher, was down and breathing extremely hard. I arrived to find the mare in the first stages of delivery. I watched from the doorway for a few seconds and realized that she was having difficulty giving birth. I could see one hoof and a nose, but no second hoof. I entered her stall and knelt down beside her, offering her comforting words in an effort to get closer without frightening her. With my heart beating rapidly, I gently reached for the other hoof and immediately found it. Once in position, the foal came fairly quickly.

As I sat there, the mare stood and looked down at her new foal, which was not moving. I rubbed him vigorously, and still he lay there lifeless on the floor of the stall. Dusty stood at the door of the stall while Garrett played in the next stall, which was empty.

"Do something!" Dusty cried with the same anguish in her voice as I must have had the night Garrett was born. I really wasn't completely sure what to do, but I noticed a tear in the sac and kept tearing it more until the tiny foal's face was exposed. I took the towels that we had kept in the barn and wiped his nose and mouth and rubbed him vigorously once again; still nothing. The mare began pawing at the foal trying to get him up as he lay there perfectly still. I could see the anguish in her eyes; it was the same anguish that I saw in my daughter's eyes that cold snowy night when Garrett was born and not breathing. I knew I had to do something. I wiped the foal's nose and mouth again and placed my mouth over his and breathed gently. I did this three or four times, praying as I had done on that night when Garrett was born.

Just when I was ready to give up, the foal moved slightly. He moved again and then he took a deep breath and opened his eyes. As he struggled to his feet, he staggered a bit, but he was alive. I had breathed life into another living creature, and I witnessed his first breath on his own. I had not only witnessed the miracle of birth, but I had actually taken part in it! I had felt so helpless when Garrett was born, and when Charlie lost her foals (and later when she died, I thought of Teddy and how it hurt me to find the grace to let him go). I had had no control over their fate, and yet there, sitting on the floor of that stall watching the mare nuzzle her new baby, I didn't feel helpless. I felt empowered by my ability to change his fate, and I felt grateful to God for allowing me to help his hand. More than anything, I was happy that Dusty was there, because she better understood how difficult it was to feel so helpless, and then to feel the joy of knowing that everything is all right. We brought Garrett in to see the new foal, and then we called the vet to come and check him out.

In the days that followed, there were many setbacks in the foal's condition. His legs were crooked due to his awkward position in the womb; he was breathing from his abdomen because his lungs were compromised. It took several hours to get him to nurse, but even with all the complications, he made it through. His legs straightened, his lungs began to expand and contract normally, and he grew to be strong, healthy, and beautiful. I spent the next four months playing with him and entertaining the option of keeping him; however, I knew he would move on to a home of his own. Our place in their lives is to see to it that they get the best start possible, and we had done that. Then we are responsible for finding them the best home possible, and we did that. My friends Dave and Kathy from Vermont drove down and claimed the colt for their own. I was sad to see him leave, as I watched him calmly step up into their trailer for his long trip home. I cried as they pulled down the driveway, but I knew that he was in excellent hands. Kathy named him Sparky, and he is the love of her life.

The miracle of birth is more than just something to observe; it is a lifetime of responsibility to that new person or animal. It is a bond that will last forever, and, although I want to keep every baby that is born here each year, I know that isn't practical. Sparky strengthened the bond between my daughter and me, and he taught me that between birth and death, there is so much more than regretting the past or anticipating the future. There are all of the precious moments that lie in between. Savor every one of them.

Chapter Twenty-Two
Hootie

Survival

*E*very lesson I've ever learned from my horses was put to the ultimate test in this final story. It is so much more about people than it is about horses, but it is also about overcoming the greatest obstacle that we, as a family, have ever had to face. As I've said from the beginning, every morning when I go out to my barn, I am given a gift. The gift that horses give me is peace in my life and strength to overcome whatever challenge I must face. They have taught me to love without reservation and to give of myself without regret; to forgive and to move on with my life; and to have faith in God and in myself when all hope seems lost. They have taught me to look at a situation with greater perspective, and they remind me to look deeper inside my own soul to find the answers to the most difficult questions. More than anything else, the horses that I have loved have taught me how to survive.

One hot July day, Bear and I were at home working on a project, when suddenly he called for me. When I entered the room, he was pale and shaking and confused. He told me that he needed to go to the hospital because he didn't know where he was. It was determined that he had suffered three strokes. Within a week, he was diagnosed with sub-acute bacterial endocarditis, which is an infection in the lining of his heart. The doctors believed that the infection spread from a tooth that he had recently had pulled, and that the infection had traveled to his heart, his spine, and his brain. He had to undergo open-heart surgery to replace the aortic and mitral valves in his heart with metal ones, and then they would need to place a permanent pacemaker, because his heart had become incapable of beating on its own. At 47 years old, we were told that it was quite possible that he would not make it through surgery, much less survive for any length of time following surgery.

We had been together every day for twenty-five years, and now I was faced with losing my best friend, the one person who knew me better than I knew myself. The strength that is required to hold a family together during such a difficult time is more strength than I ever knew I had. Jennifer still lived at home, and she was with me every day. She returned phone calls and kept people up to date on Bear's condition. The two of us took turns sitting for endless hours by his bedside in the hospital, and when we brought him home, we took turns caring for him and giving him medication every day during the weeks that followed. She never let me down once during this time. It was so incredibly difficult to stay on top of everything that needed to be done, and my daughter—the person with whom I had spent endless hours at horse shows and 4-H meetings—was right there beside me throughout the entire ordeal. I would not have gotten through those long months without her. When things became almost too much to bear, we would keep each other's spirits up by asking the other if Oprah had called. It was a joke that never failed to make us laugh. On her TV show, we had seen Oprah Winfrey help so many people who needed it, and we needed help so badly.

After several months of rehabilitation and endless doctors and nurses coming and going at the house, we were all drained emotionally, financially, and spiritually, but Bear was still alive and we would hold on to that. Shortly after this occurred and he was recovering, it was discovered that one of the valves in his heart was too small, and, according to the operative report, although the surgeon had measured the area for a 27mm valve, a 23mm valve had been placed instead. The result was that he was in congestive heart failure and had to undergo a second open-heart surgery and start the painful process of recovery all over again. He was also told that riding or working around horses would be out of the question because he would be on blood thinners the rest of his life, and it was too dangerous; we couldn't risk any injury because he could possibly bleed out before he ever got to a hospital. Bear was in the hospital for a week while we waited for a different surgeon to be available for consultation before performing the second surgery. With each day that passed, he became sicker and more depressed at his prospects. One day, after a long stretch at the hospital, I came home in tears. I needed to go out to the barn and just be alone for a while. The phone was ringing off the hook, there were people coming and going, there were bills that could not get paid, and I felt at the end of my proverbial rope.

Hootie is a buckskin gelding and one of our stallion's babies. His mom is Cher, my favorite mare, so Hootie is my idea of the perfect horse. I sat on the ground with my back against one of the small barns and cried. I prayed for an answer to this dilemma, and I prayed for the strength to help Bear get through this. I tried to understand why it was happening and how I would ever survive life without the man I loved. He was my best friend, and he was dying. I didn't trust the same surgeon to perform the second open-heart surgery, and yet we had to wait for the other doctor to return. What if we were making a mistake by waiting, and what if the choices we made would cause him to die? I questioned everything I had done until that point, and everything I was as a wife and a human being in general. My confidence was gone, my faith was shaken, and for just a brief moment, I wanted to die. I didn't have the strength to get up and go on and help my husband, and I hated myself for that, but I couldn't move. I felt as I had that long-ago day in the meadow, frightened of the storm and covering my eyes and mouth so the dragonflies wouldn't sew them shut. It was a paralyzing fear. I tried to reassure myself, as Rex Wiley had assured me when I was a child, that the dragonflies were my spiritual guides and they were there to protect me, but there were no dragonflies to be seen on this day, and there was no one to protect me from what was happening.

The sun was sinking into the west, and the cool breeze offered a welcome relief from the searing heat. I sat there with my eyes closed, the sun on my face, and suddenly I felt a presence. I opened my eyes, and Hootie was standing over me. He began nudging me, and I pushed him away. He nudged harder, and I hollered at him to go away, but he didn't. He stood his ground until the nudging gave me no choice but to stand. When I did, he came to me and placed his head on my chest. I knew that this wonderful, intelligent creature was feeling my pain. I stroked his soft black mane and traced the line around his eyes with my fingertips, and it suddenly became clear to me what I had to do. The answer was there, I had just been too tired and frightened to see it. I knew that these horses had carried us through the toughest times in our lives and now when we needed the lessons that they taught the most, I had turned my back on them.

I woke the next morning ready to put my plan into action. Bear had been lying in a hospital bed for a week after several months of rehabilitation before that. I walked into his hospital room with determination. I told the nurses that I was taking him outside. They said that the doctors would not allow it. I told them to "tell" the doctors that he needed to go outside, and we would be back in a while. I figured that I could continue to sit around and wait for him to either die from his condition or from the mistakes that were made, or I could give him hope and the strength to face what lay ahead.

Once outside, I told Bear to close his eyes and turn to the east so the sun was on his face. He was too depressed, but I was too determined for him to refuse. When the sun touched his face, he smiled. For the first time in months, he smiled! I leaned in and kissed his cheek and whispered to him, "You are standing on our back deck, and it is the perfect summer day. It is early in the morning, and everything is the way it was before all of this happened. You are looking out onto green pastures filled with our horses. There are babies playing beside their mothers, and Beau is looking up at the house and calling for you to come out to the barn." Bear smiled again and even in his weakened state, he looked genuinely happy. The deep creases in his forehead softened as he let go of the stress of the situation.

"You are a survivor!" I continued empathically. "Nothing—not this illness, not any medical mistake, nothing—is ever going to take you away from me. Do you understand me?" I asked through my tears. He nodded and continued to keep his eyes closed for a few more moments. For the first time in so long, I saw a look of peace and comfort come over his face. "We will get through this together," I reminded him, and he nodded again.

Everything changed after that day. Bear survived the second open-heart surgery, and although there will always be challenges ahead for us, we will face them together because we are survivors, he and I; our horses taught us that. Hootie gave me the strength that day to get up when I had completely given up on everything. He gave me the strength to take care of my family during the darkest time in our lives. Although none of us lives forever and death is inevitable, our horses have taught us that life is more about quality than quantity. It is about living well, not living long. They have taught us that it is in each moment that we find our greatest happiness, and that there is so much more to living than regretting the past or anticipating the future. It is about the here and now, the perfect summer days filled with joy and happiness, and the magical winter snowstorms that fill the sky with lightning. In the darkest days in your life, it is the ability to close your eyes and feel the warmth of the sun on your face and allow your imagination to take you to a better place. It is the pure joy of galloping without reservation across an open field on the back of a horse who takes your breath away.

The lessons we've learned from horses we've loved for all these years gave us both the strength to survive every heartbreaking moment of Bear's illness and the hope and faith to see it through. When I was young and realized after a tornado came through that bad things sometimes happen and that our lives can change so quickly, I was incredibly frightened. Then I met Dewey, and he taught me that I was capable of dealing with the sudden changes and the devastation in my life. Harley and Star taught my family to fully appreciate the second chances that we are given in life. Charlie made us stronger through a lesson of facing adversity and getting through the most difficult times.

Eve, the Mexican pony, Teddy—all of our horses were there with us through the darkest days. The lessons we learned from them made us the people we are today, people who survive and are given a second chance. We are a family that thanks God that we have had the privilege of knowing and learning from these noble creatures. Most of all, we are grateful for the opportunity to share those lessons with you.

Reflections

Through these pages, I have taken you on a journey into a life filled with some of the horses that I have loved and the lessons that I have learned from them. I have witnessed interaction between horse and human that has left me with such a deep feeling of sympathy that it has reduced me to tears—not only for the abused and neglected horse, but also for the human who seems to lack an understanding or connection to these beautiful creatures. I have also witnessed the excitement of a person who understands this connection and is realizing for the first time all the wonder that it brings. It fills my spirit with a childlike renewal of the first time I ever saw a horse or how much I appreciate the smell of a freshly bathed horse as he dries in the sun; the sound of thundering hooves as they run to meet me at the gate after a day out in the pasture. It reminds me again of how peaceful it can be to lay in a hammock under a glorious blue sky on a warm summer day and watch horses interact with each other and with their surroundings.

Being as involved with horses as I have been for so many years, I have heard the term *horse whisperer* used repeatedly. Although I do believe that some of us actually "feel" what an animal feels, I don't believe it is anything more than pure compassion. To me, looking into the eyes of a horse is like looking into a mirror of your own soul. They reflect that which cannot be explained; that which cannot be found anywhere else.

Through loving these incredible horses, I have had the privilege of learning so much about life and how to live it better, and about love and how to give it without reservation. I have learned that nothing lasts forever, so we must appreciate the here and now and not lose sight of its value by focusing on the past or future.

Your life is a gift, and the more you treasure every moment and appreciate every person who touches it along the way, the better your life will be. Be good to the people you love, but remember to be good to yourself as well. Give your spirit wings by allowing yourself the joy of unleashing your inner child now and then. Find joy in the simplest of tasks, and when it comes time to perform a task that you don't necessarily enjoy, find simple ways to make it more fun. Allow yourself to mow the lawn wearing gold Elvis sunglasses or go trick-or-treating in full costume. I find that a pair of shiny red cowboy boots can make me feel good about myself, regardless of what I'm doing or how I feel. Always remember that you are no good to anyone else unless you are first good to yourself.

My job as a writer is to inspire you, and the purpose of writing this particular book is to inspire you to find joy and laughter and balance in your life; to realize that you are everything that my horses inspire *me* to be. Remember that you have the ability to change a life with a mere word, so choose your words wisely and always back them up with a smile. Wake each morning genuinely excited about the possibilities of the day ahead of you, and go to bed each night knowing that you have squeezed every possible ounce of living out of that day. Never give up on your dreams, and never allow anyone else to tell you that your dream is impossible. When it comes to possibly losing someone you love, fight for every moment together and cherish it for as long as you can. Be willing to forgive another for his or her mistakes and shortcomings, and know that we all evolve at a different pace. Because of this, there is always something you can learn and something you can teach.

Know that you are a survivor, and remind yourself of that when things become almost too difficult to bear. Regardless of what your faith allows you to believe, have faith in something and know that when that faith is challenged the most is when it will become the strongest. If you are blessed with the joy of horses in your life, then you know that very little can compare to watching a newborn foal take his first breath or walking out to your barn in the early morning light and feeling the presence of these awesome creatures. If you have never experienced the pleasure of horses, I hope that you someday get the opportunity to look into their eyes at the reflection of your own soul. Above all else, I pray that the lessons that these horses have taught me, that I share with you in this book, will lead you to a better life filled with hope and happiness.